Monk
in the
Market Place

and the Simpsons

Monk
in the
Market Place

and the Simpsons

My autobiography

RAY SIMPSON

DARTON·LONGMAN+TODD

First published in Great Britain in 2021 by
Darton, Longman and Todd Ltd
1 Spencer Court
140–142 Wandsworth High Street
London SW18 4JJ

© 2021 Ray Simpson

ISBN: 978-1-913657-05-5

A catalogue record for this book is available from the British Library.

Phototypeset by Kerrypress Limited, St Albans Herts.
Printed and bound by Bell & Bain, Glasgow.

Before I formed you in the womb I knew you ...
... his word is in my heart like a fire, a fire shut up in my bones.
I am weary of holding it in; indeed, I cannot.

Jeremiah 1:5 and 20:9

Embody me.
Flare up like flame
And make big shadows I can move in.

Rainer Maria Rilke

Contents

Acknowledgements

I thank the following:

My sister Sally for reading and revising a draft script; Graham Booth for reading and revising the chapter on Holy Island; Peter Neilson for reading and revising the chapters on Holy Island and Borderlands; my relatives Jane, Jo, Fr Ken, Sam, Kemi and Peter for revising relevant paragraphs about the Simpsons; my secretary Brenda for countless corrections; Melanie for keeping my house beautifully clean while I concentrate on writing; Carol for helping with send-outs; Charles for his memorable foreword; my endorsers; and David and colleagues at DLT for their unstinting helpfulness.

Foreword

by Charles Nienkirchen, PhD Professor Emeritus of Christian History and Spirituality, Ambrose University Calgary Alberta, Canada

Autobiography should try to tell the truth about one's life journey. *Monk in the Marketplace* is a compelling account of a decades-long quest for God inflamed by spiritual yearning. It speaks honestly of personal psychological foibles, relational complexities, complicated circumstances difficult to navigate, mistakes made and costly sacrifices. At times, the author's pain registers just beneath the text. Moreover, vocational clarity for him is found as much in the messy nooks and crannies of life as in some easily discerned, grand design. The author extends generous affirmation to myriad others who have made formative contributions to shaping his life narrative.

A deep, faithful commitment to the work of the church is evident throughout, but it is also a fidelity marked by a resolute refusal to be defined by the historic divisions and strictures of the institutional church. A penchant for scandalously bold, innovative ecumenism discloses genuine respect for the laudable contributions of a broad latitude of Christian traditions. It frames a spiritual entrepreneurship punctuated with adventurous risk-taking, that with its celebrated successes has not been immune to the flickerings of faith spawned by opposition, misunderstanding and disappointments. Nevertheless, even in his senior years his advocacy of unity within and beyond the church remains undaunted.

Told with meticulous detail, this inspired story captures the imagination with frequent flowerings of human creativity amidst the grind that invariably comes with a life of service. It also shows deference to the mysteries of the invisible, spiritual world revealed through charisms of the Holy Spirit. The author experiences an animated Christianity that goes beyond rationalism and dogma.

He takes nature, dreams and visions seriously as frequencies for the divine voice. For him, such suprarational phenomena draw attention to the immanence of the spiritual world. A kind, divine hand, though difficult to discern at times, superintends life and guides all things through chaos and order alike. His sense of the significance of his own life is also informed and nourished by the comings and goings of the generations of Simpsons in his family tree who stand behind the thin veil of time.

As he matured, the author's commitment deepened to life as a pilgrimage of wandering and witness beyond the restrictions of religious convention. He often departed his tidally protected refuge on the Holy Island of Lindisfarne to export across the western world a Celtic message of renewal for individuals, churches and creation. Invitational speaking and a prolific flow of publications and electronic communications has birthed an international constituency. His prayer-dependent, faith-fuelled life has esteemed relationships over institutions evidenced in the network of supportive friends and colleagues that has aided and abetted his 'Celtic Revivalist' cause into the third millennium.

Western Christendom is dying. In its place the author anchors his message of renewal in an earlier, more pristine era of Christian history. He has garnered fresh hope for the salvation of the world from the prominent male and female personalities, teachings and wisdom of Celtic Christian antiquity. He finds in Celtic theology, spirituality and missional enterprise, a convergent Christianity capable of recovering Christ from the Catholic and Protestant versions of Christendom. They transformed the structure and message of the church in an imperial manner at odds with the demeanour and intent of the faith's founder. The author envisions a more humble and simple living church that warmly welcomes indigenous peoples and ends their colonial oppression. In this vein he has revived the model of the intentional community known to Celtic monastics. In its disciplined life under a common rule he sees a way forward for authentic Christ following amidst the embers of Christendom.

In the summer of 2011 I arrived on Lindisfarne with a group of students retracing the footsteps of the Celtic saints. Unexpectedly, a memorable encounter with Ray Simpson awaited. Late on a misty island night he invited me to Starbank Cottage, his retreat residence. As a veteran, Celtic-styled soulfriend, he reached out with disarming conversational hospitality. Instant mutual trust enabled us to speak to each other unreservedly. His words morphed effortlessly into prophetic speech with layers of personal significance. He first discerned the vocational joy I derive from being an itinerant professor. Wise counsel ensued recommending the appropriate response to a toxic set of circumstances in my life of which he had no prior knowledge. Lastly, he encouraged me to recognize this as the time to leave ego behind so that the true self could emerge. Such was my serendipitous baptism into spiritual direction done the Celtic way.

The author, though practising a gentler asceticism, is nonetheless a spiritual heir of the ancient Celtic Christians. Over several decades, he has exuded the same fortitude of heart seen in the Celtic monks who abandoned themselves in their fragile, skinned coracles to perilous ocean currents that providentially guided them to an unknown destination where they found their resurrection.

From a War-Time Womb

It is only out of this matrix, this womb, that something wonderful and new in history can be born.

Aylesbury

My parents got their timing wrong. They conceived me in June 1939, three months before Herr Hitler declared war on Britain. I had three months of bliss in the womb before their lives, and mine, were shattered. Three decades later I discovered, during a primal therapy week, that following the bliss of the first womb trimester I suddenly became hysterical and uncontrollable.

So the memory of much of my infant life is blocked out. I can recall only a few fragments. I know I was born on 9 March 1940 in Aylesbury Hospital, Buckinghamshire, in England. My parents and elder brother Tony lived in Vine Cottage, Aylesbury. When war broke out, my maternal grandparents, Joseph and Sarah Todhunter, were evacuated from London bomb-threat zones, and squeezed into Vine Cottage. My father's asthmatic elder sister Mattie and her husband John at first allowed incorrigible Granddad Simpson to stay with them, but they soon sent him packing to co-exist with the Todhunters and the rest of us. Granddad Simpson was a cantankerous loner, though looking back I also think he was a flawed hero. This dysfunctional family were like sardines in a small tin.

The last thing they needed was a new baby. I was squeezed into some small space with no electric lights lest Hitler's bombers would see us. I recall feeling frightened when my lone night light flickered out. I was in the way. Maybe I wished I had never been born. An unconscious desire grew in me to get back into that warm, safe mother's womb.

My father, Frederick Alexander Simpson, was not called up for military duty. I do not know why. He was a senior accountant for the publishing firm Hazel, Watson and Viney. Was this too important a job to forego for war service? He was, however, drafted into the Home Guard (the 'Dad's Army' of the war years). He was always tense, and was often absent on duty at weekends. The only foods I can remember are packets of dried egg powder and dried bananas.

Apart from the night-light, just two memories come through the void of those first years. I recall the first time I was allowed to place two lumps of sugar in my hand, hold it out flat, and let a horse lick them up. I tingled with delight. The animal world had none of the repression of my world of humans. Was this my first intimation that we are designed for communion with creation, which is free from prejudice? The second memory would have been beyond recall, were it not for a photograph I found in an album. We had no holidays during the war, but towards the end, when it was clear Hitler could not win, my father took me to a guest cottage in Windsor Forest. During the war there were no gifts for sale, but the woman who ran this B&B made stuffed dolls from old rags. This was the first time I became aware that it was possible to buy a present, even for a few pence. The photo features my father kneeling, with me and a dog playing. My father never played with me after that. So that photo stood in for a thousand missed play times. It contains a glimpse of a lost paradise – a forest, a dog, and a parent at play.

Woking – God calling

Before the war officially ended my parents managed to buy a bungalow in Westfield Avenue, Woking. This Surrey town has some countryside (H.G. Wells sited his *War of the Worlds* at Horsell, near

Woking's six crossroads) but is mainly a place from which people commute to London. At one end of Westfield Avenue is Woking Football Club and Seventh Woking Scouts headquarters. Near the other end were Westfield Infants and Westfield Junior Schools. The avenue was not tarmacked (it had large puddles) and we could walk to nearby common land.

My elder brother Tony and I each had to sleep in a steel cage with iron netting on one side. A bomb once dropped in a field not far away, but we generally felt safe. When the war was over our neighbour Mrs Gilbert, organized a victory party. Tables lined the street, festooned with balloons, and we ate endless jellies and cakes which these ladies somehow summoned from thin air. A famous concert singer (I nick-named her Madame de Lara Pom Pom) opened the event. This was my first experience of a party.

I went to Westfield Infants School. I only remember two events. My first girlfriend, I announced, was called Rosemary. During break times we sat together under a tree in the middle of the playground holding hands. I can't remember my teachers. Except for one, who died in the floods at Lynton in Devon, while she was on holiday.

When I was seven my mother gave birth to my sister, Sally. My parents said they had not planned to have a third child but they were clearly delighted that they had, and that she was a girl. Whereas I had to make do with second-hand clothing handed on from my brother, everything she had was new!

My life felt like a sandwich. I was sandwiched between an elder brother who had new clothes and found his feet before war broke out, and a younger sister who escaped the 'sardine tin existence' of war-time and was born in a period when our parents could afford to cherish her. I began to ask my mother questions such as: 'Am I really your child or did you adopt me?' and 'Did you really want me?' She assured me I was wanted and was not adopted, but her words did not fully undo the negative message within me.

After three years I moved on to Westfield Junior School. The Head Mistress was Miss Holmes, and her Deputy was Miss Urmston. I only remember two things about that school. The first was when our geography teacher – Mr Skeet – said that our mothers were saints. I was astonished. Two worlds that were a million miles apart in my mind – saints and home – were suddenly brought together.

The second memory was about two boys who used to bully me. They waited for me after school and made me give them piggy backs. I mostly hid my emotions at home, because Dad was bad tempered and I was frightened of opening up my feelings in case his words hurt me. But the bullying reached such a pitch that my parents found me crying, and reported it to the headmistress. She was wise. She wanted to stop the bullying, but she also wanted me to stand up for myself. So she told me to wait until they bullied me inside the playground; then I must stand up to them, so the teachers could witness it and then deal with it. I did stand up to them. Half the school and the teachers gathered round to watch the fight. They never bullied me again. This taught me a great lesson.

I was bottled up, and occasionally this spilled over into outbursts of rage. Once I threw across the room the hot meal my mum had lovingly prepared. It hurt me to hurt her, but it made a statement, though I did not know why I was so angry.

I teamed up with Raymond Clayton, the boy next door, whom I suspect was also emotionally blocked. Once we set fire to the common. We ran down the street shouting, 'Fire, fire!' and hid under some rabbit hutches to avoid being caught by the police. On another occasion we ran away. We missed two meals and hid under a bridge by the river. But eventually, cold and dark caused us to return home. Another statement had been made. On a third occasion I locked myself in the bathroom so that no one could use the toilet.

This behaviour might in part be explained by the fact that my father came home late, smoked heavily, was tense and emotionally unavailable. Yet there was one occasion when I realized that deep down he did care about me. I tripped on a bush and broke my arm in two places. My father accompanied me to the hospital in a mini-ambulance. Every time it went over a bump he winced and shouted things to the driver like 'Be careful'.

I was unhappy at both the schools I went to. At play times I did not join in games, I leaned against the school wall. I became somewhat plump. They called me Jumbo. Because I was emotionally blocked, the teachers said I could do better. Some inchoate drive deep within me also knew that I could do better. One term before we sat the 'eleven-plus' exams which would determine who would qualify to go to a grammar school, I gave priority attention to schoolwork, leapt up the 'league table', and passed.

That is why in September 1951 I joined Woking Grammar School for Boys. The only non-male teacher was Miss Bottom, a stern matriarch who glared at us as we entered the classroom and said nothing until there was complete silence. We called her 'Ma Bot'.

My parents had moved up in the world by this time. We had left the Westfield Avenue bungalow for a house in Cavendish Road. My sister went to a nearby Montessori school. I started piano lessons with a Christian Scientist woman down the road. Eventually, I gained a grade seven. I remember playing Mozart's Moonlight Sonata, but I could never manage Bach's Fugue in D Minor.

Sometime around then I, like my brother Tony, joined the Seventh Woking Boy Scout Troop. I remember cycling to Scouts with Tony in the rain. He said, 'You are dripping' – a double entendre, I thought. I was dripping wet and my plump body was like dripping fat. He left the troop and I stayed on. I became a patrol leader, gained the First-Class Award (which included map reading and camping out at night), and ended up as Troop Leader. With my low self-image I could not imagine why. This low self-image was buttressed when I led my patrol on a trek. They did not believe my map-reading and left me to plough on alone. I got chased by a bull, and arrived back long after everyone else. I was so ashamed that I covered myself in wet mud to re-direct attention from my inner to my outer being. Half the world seems to do that nowadays. In contrast to this I was rather proud (Oh, foolish youth!) that I won an unofficial competition for the scout who could stand on a fire longest!

My boyhood had emerged among the embers of the British Empire. I remember India and then Rhodesia, re-named Zimbabwe, gaining their independence. I was growing up into a new global framework.

My father was 'emotionally' in London, where he had set up his own accountancy firm with a partner. He came home late, was tense and irritable, and usually shut himself in the lounge smoking and, latterly, watching TV. He was a member of London's famous Wig and Pen Club, a haunt for writers, lawyers and raconteurs. He dabbled in writing as a hobby, including subjects such as Mithras remains in London. We heard about his special writer friend, who was called Lorna. Whether he had an affair with her, or with others, I can only surmise.

My mother was placid, kind, and a Methodist, like her parents. The Todhunters had moved to Winchmore Hill, London, from the Lake District. Mother was a fan of Dr Leslie Weatherhead, a liberal Methodist. She took us to the Methodist Church. I went to its Sunday School. Mr Fosbury taught us – but such a sublime doctrine as the Third Person of the Holy Trinity entirely escaped me. I had a dream in which the said Mr Fosbury chased me with a prickly bunch of holly. 'It's the Holly Ghost!', I screamed as I awoke from my nightmare. I did not get to know the Holy Spirit at Woking Methodist Church, and my parents permitted me to cease my attendance.

I avoided my father's company, and lingered with my mother in the kitchen long after washing up should have been completed. Christmas was the one occasion which half broke the mould. We gathered at Auntie Mattie's with Uncle John and Cousin Kenneth, and played charades. They lived at Jacob's Well, Guildford, and then moved to Worthing.

I was too shy to make proper friends at school. A fellow student named Ossie lived nearby, and big John Orridge had a warm heart. I felt a connection with them but was too introverted to know how to develop a real relationship. As for girls, they were non-existent. A single-sex school was not helpful for me.

One day I apologized to Barny, the Assistant Scout leader, for reading the wrong prayer at the end of a Scout meeting. He said, 'Do you want to know what prayer is really about? Come for a cycle ride and I will tell you'. We cycled to a river. He said, 'If you drowned in that river what would happen to you?' I said, 'I'd be dead'. He said, 'You'd go to hell. But if you ask Jesus Christ into your life you will be saved. Do you want to ask him?' I said something like, 'I think so.' Barny said 'You can either go to the tree over there and ask him in yourself, or I can pray on your behalf'. I chose the tree, and asked Jesus into my life.

Scoffers may say that I had no idea what I was doing. Looking back, I picture my life as a house with many rooms. I let Jesus through the front door but kept the doors to the rooms shut. Jesus remained firmly shut out of my sexuality and out of my home. In spite of this, he now had a foothold, and a profoundly significant and life-changing journey had begun. My conversion may have been immature and un-whole, my behaviour and my emotions were often un-Christian, my constructs false, yet from that time, and ever since, I have sensed that Jesus was accompanying me, like The Hound of Heaven in Francis Thompson's poem:

> *I fled Him, down the nights and down the days;*
> *I fled Him, down the arches of the years;*
> *I fled Him, down the labyrinthine ways*
> *Of my own mind; and in the midst of tears*
> *I hid from Him, and under running laughter…*

> *'Ah, fondest, blindest, weakest,*
> *I am He Whom thou seekest!*
> *Thou dravest love from thee, who dravest Me.'*

What church should I join? Barny was a Baptist. I already went to the Scouts monthly parade service at St Mary of Bethany Church of England. I liked the sense of history and of liturgy in the Church of England, so that became my church. I was baptized at the age of thirteen, along with five adults who had gone forward to accept Christ at evangelist Billy Graham's rallies at London's Haringey Arena, which I also attended.

Barny enrolled me at the Crusaders Bible Class (later, Crusaders were re-named Urban Saints). I took the Bible seriously. I learned evangelical choruses there which I shall probably recall on my death bed, when other more erudite memories have faded:

Thou art the potter, I am the clay. Mould me and make me, in thine own way. Whatever the vessel, grant me to be, used in thy service to glorify thee.

Keep me shining, Lord, keep me shining, Lord, in all I say and do; that the world may see Christ lives in me and learn to love him too.

In my fourth year at Woking Grammar School I helped to start a Christian Union. I only gained five O levels in my fifth year, but these were enough for me to stay on in the sixth form to study History, English and a little Latin.

I still under-performed in studies and team sports. A constant refrain in my termly school reports was 'He could do better'. Yet occasionally ambition overcame my poor motivation. The school plays had a fine reputation as almost professional productions: I played leading roles in two of them – Shakespeare's *Richard II* and a Terence Rattigan play. The School Declamation Trophy required the winner to declaim on one of several given subjects. The winner had to repeat part of it in front of parents and students at the annual school prize-giving. I found myself declaiming at the prize-giving on the subject (quoting from John Milton) 'Let not England forget her precedence of teaching nations how to live'. I spoke with great passion and moral earnestness. I still have the text, written by hand in a red notebook. It begins, 'Mr Headmaster, Sir, members of staff, school …' and it ends, 'During the eighteenth-century rise of capitalism, man came to take his laws, not from God, but from the money-lenders. All free nations have fought to destroy the materialistic tyrannies arising from this. It was England that first, unconsciously, led the world into this morass: England must discover the way out. (Quick bow – finis).'

I blush now to recall the arrogant colonialism implicit in this declamation, but perhaps beneath the arrogance was a passion for the world to know 'some word of truth' such as Solzhenitsyn would expound years later.

Puberty

What happened when puberty began? The most colossal repression of an outsize sex drive. My conversion did not touch it. I read 'naughty' comics in secret. One year I became a skinhead and cycled shirtless with a group of lads, but generally I was frightened to reveal my masculinity. I would have loved to join a boxing club, but instead held back in the school gym and on the sports fields, and was jealous of a class-mate named Chris who developed and displayed rippling muscles. I was untalented at team games that required good co-ordination but I did take up running. I recall masturbating when I overtook the person I emulated most during a cross-country running race.

A vast amount of testosterone was released in me. The sex drive felt like a runaway horse. I was terrified of it. My conversion had no effect upon this. I fantasized that I would spend a secret week-end in a Paris brothel, return and live a moral, Christ-centered life ever after; no one would ever know about my fling. But I still had no feeling for girls. If I had gone to a brothel it would have been cheap, loveless, exploitative, ignorant and failed sex – or would it have awakened something?

During and after puberty I was emotionally unintelligent and often behaved like a bull in a china shop. However, one day I read in my Bible, 'If any of you lacks wisdom, let him ask from God, the One giving generously to all and not finding fault, and it will be given to him': James 1:5. I asked for wisdom. All I can claim is that I am less unwise than I otherwise would be.

I had to share a bedroom with my elder brother at this time. This I resented. One day I hit him with a poker, and on another day I peed into the glass from which he drank water. I was not nice. He was an atheist until one day I gave him a book by Dr Jim Packer entitled *Fundamentalism and the Word of God*. This changed his life and I think he followed its tenets ever after. He attended a network of evangelical meetings in Woking that I had introduced him to. He eschewed military duties during his two years of National Service, on pacifist grounds, and instead undertook mental health duties.

Should I become a communist? A new call

In the sixth form I became gripped by Bible stories of God-guided personalities who shaped their country, but I became disillusioned with Bible class Christians who talked about Jesus as a passport to heaven but who made no impact on this world. I read Chairman Mao's *Little Red Book*, which called for a ceaseless revolution of unselfishness (his selfish brutality had not yet been revealed). I became gripped by Communists who had a philosophy, plan and passion to change the world. I questioned Christianity. Should I become an atheist? I was also confused as to what career I should pursue when I left school – I toyed with being a boxer, a politician, a journalist or a farmer – so I decided to try an experiment. One Good Friday, I knelt for three hours and prayed, 'O God, if there is a God, show me what you want me to be and I will do what you want for the rest of my life'.

On the following Bank Holiday Monday, I cycled with a friend to a youth fellowship dance in a venue we had never been to. We got lost in a thick fog, and agreed to ask directions from the next person we saw – which would have to be directly under a streetlight. This was a wrinkled old lady. She gave us directions, asked a few questions, looked me in the eyes and said, 'Young man, the Lord is calling you to full-time ministry for him. I was called to be a missionary, but ill-health prevented it. The mantle the Lord put on me I now put on you.' She walked off into the fog and we never saw her again.

'Nobody in my family is like that,' I told my friend, 'no one is ordained.' 'You idiot', he said, 'I can tell you six people who think you should be ordained.' The steps towards that, however, became messy. The Church of England advised that I should go to university, get some work experience, and then apply for ordination appraisal. However, I failed the history exam that would have ensured me a university place, and instead of re-sitting it at Woking Grammar School I had to move to West Sussex with my family.

Before leaving I attended a packed new year meeting addressed by the industrialist Sir John Laing, who was President of London Bible College. He challenged us not to burn out prematurely for

God as a result of over-activism, but to let our lives be like a gentle candle that consistently burns daily until every bit of its wax is used and it gently flickers out after a long life. I dedicated myself to be like that candle flame, a life-long flame for God.

Sussex

My father got fed up doing a job he had never liked. He asked his partner to manage his half of his London accountancy firm, and purchased Burlington Lounge, a loss-making regency coffee shop in the main shopping street of Bognor Regis. He hoped to turn around its fortunes by removing the grand piano and introducing meals. We could not afford to live in Bognor Regis, so I found myself stranded in a collection of houses called Westergate, eleven miles away, devoid of transport or a career plan.

My sister Sally went to Bognor Regis Grammar School on the bus and flourished. On completing her studies she went to Jamaica with VSO (Voluntary Service Overseas) for two years. My brother went to Brighton School of Art, though after his conversion he burned all his paintings (some of them very good), because he thought they were idols, projections of his unredeemed self, and he transferred to the Pentecostal International Bible Training Institute at Burgess Hill, Sussex. There he met and married Agnete, from Denmark. They read a booklet entitled *In Darkest Ireland* (the darkness was Roman Catholicism as it was then), and felt God was calling them to start a Pentecostal ministry in the Republic of Ireland's second city of Cork, named The Upper Room. It began with one or two people meeting in a rat-infested room in the city centre. It expanded to include a day centre.

I, in contrast to my brother and sister, wondered whether I was going nowhere. In fact, I was starting at the bottom of a divine learning school. During this time I acquired an empathy for the people at the bottom of the social mobility scale who were unemployed or who were confined to hard but unsatisfying jobs or who were marginalized because of race or class. This has stayed with me throughout my life.

A local ordinand named John Morrison urged me to visit a nearby vicar and ask his advice as to whether I should pursue ordination. 'You do know that you will have to wear a black suit for the rest of your life' the vicar told me. That was a big put-down, but I survived it – just! I was accepted for ordination in the Church of England, but advised to get work experience and a GCSE in Religious Studies before I started theological college. So I acquired a scooter and began an unforgettable two-year kaleidoscope of job experiences.

My father said I would be a businessman, and I certainly developed a talent for selling things. I got a job selling encyclopedias. To buy the multi-volumes was a big investment. I sensed that the Windrush Generation who had arrived in England from the Caribbean had a passion to further their education. I convinced one such man that to buy these encyclopedias was the way to fufil his ambition. He invested in it even though he could not afford it. Yes, I was a successful capitalist, but my conscience got the better of me. I gave up that job. However, my conscience allowed me to sell the local daily newspaper twice over. I discovered that the last column was updated with the afternoon racing results, and that if I walked along the queues of seaside visitors' cars shouting 'Latest racing results!' they would buy a copy. The paper's sales beat all records!

I got a summer job at Bognor's new Butlin's Holiday Camp. The holiday staff all got the sack after so many stole large quantities of food. I was re-interviewed and got the job back because they concluded that I was honest. It raises the question as to whether society can function without honesty.

I delivered sacks of coal with a friendly but foul-mouthed Irish guy, taught in Etonhurst private school, cared for the bodies of physically deformed men in a care home, and worked on the shop floor of a mass production factory.

The Etonhurst headmaster caned pupils for any and every offence. He was angry that I did not. One day he got me into his study and ordered me to cane a lad, shouting at me to use more force. Today he could be prosecuted for assault. I resigned. While I was working at Lec Refrigerators' factory the workers held their first strike and I gained an A level in Religious Education. One of the young men at Ashley House Care Home spent his life laying on his front. I had to clean out the faeces from his ever-open bowels. I was changed by his sometimes long periods of non-complaining and even chirpiness.

My father achieved much at The Burlington Lounge, but not enough to bring it into profit. He threatened to open on Sundays. My mother, who worked in the kitchen, told him that would be the last straw, and she would seek a divorce if he did. I forget the exact time sequence, but the partner he had trusted to manage his clients 'took them over' without paying my father for the privilege. My father had a breakdown. So, at the age of nineteen, I became de facto manager of The Burlington Lounge. We had the best summer trade ever, with customers queuing down the stairs. On the other hand, I unwisely reduced the amount of tomato in our soups, and spilt one such soup down our best customer's jacket! In any case, my father had put the restaurant up for sale. It was one of the best things our father did. When he came to the end of his resources he handed his life over to God, lived at Westergate and began a new journey.

I decided that the church I would join would be the St Peter's, run by Church Army Captain Edmund Wilbourne on Bognor's toughest housing estate.

Theology in London: 'You see the wood but not the trees'

John Morrison urged me to visit his theological college, London College of Divinity at Northwood, and seek a place there if the local Diocese would sponsor me. How foolish I was not to master the appropriate processes, discern more clearly my own spiritual leanings, learn of the distinctive qualities of different theological colleges, and visit a range of them. LCD gave me a place. I valued the teaching on the Old Testament prophets. We had just one lecture on how to relate to social services and one on ministry to the aristocracy! Michael Green, our most well-known lecturer, perceptively told me that I could see the big picture, for example a wood, but was prone to bump into the tree in front of me! He considered I was one of the brighter students, and I was urged to spend two days a week at Kings College London doing a Bachelor of Divinity course, and to stay on for a fourth year to complete this.

Two future archbishops were on the same floor as me: Janani Luwum, who was assassinated by Uganda's dictator Idi Amin, and George Carey, who became the first working-class Archbishop of Canterbury. The College was known as St John's – in my last long vac term it moved to a new location and became St John's Nottingham. It was open evangelical in ethos. In addition to biblical and pastoral studies it tackled some other creative areas. However, I began to realize, during or after my time at college, that fundamental dimensions of life were missing such as the sacramental, social justice, community, and listening to God.

The biggest 'God thing' in my life in the course of my college years came through a 'side door' so to speak. During vacations, back at Bognor's St Peter's Tin Tabernacle, almost the only family who were not in trouble with the police were Hilda and Jim Ridgers. They followed Moral Re-Armament. This meant they had a daily quiet time, and wrote down every thought that passed the test of absolute honesty, purity, unselfishness and love. They helped at the London Moral Re-Armament bookshop.

I had promised Hilda and Jim that I would visit the MRA bookshop, at Hays Mews, before I went to college. In order to keep my promise, and feeling embarrassed, I called in on the way to my first day at college. 'I have only come because I promised the Ridgers I would', I told the bookshop lady. She fetched John, the accountant upstairs. 'My faith is sufficient, I don't need anything else', I told him, going red. 'Has your faith got an answer to your self-consciousness?' he asked. I went even more red. We chatted. 'Oh, by the way,' he said as I was leaving, 'I live at Pinner just two miles from your college, you must come for a meal.'

One term later we had the meal. 'I had the thought in my quiet time to invite you to our international conference at Caux, in Switzerland', he said. I dreaded the idea, but merely said, 'I have no money for the air ticket.' He said, 'If God wants you to go, he will provide the money.' That week, my Diocese sent its grant towards my college fees twice over. I rang the Diocese. 'We have made a mistake, but this time you can keep the extra money', said the voice. It was the exact amount of the air fare to Switzerland. Try as I did, my conscience would not let me cop out. Damn conscience!

At Caux they taught these truths: As I am, so is my nation; as my family is, so is the world. Until that conference I had no idea how the rest of the world saw the sins of the colonial British. A Chinese man, on learning I was British, said, 'Forgive me for my hatred of you. I have hated the British for inflicting the opium trade on my country.' It began to dawn on me that one can have a sense of sin not only for oneself, but for one's country or culture.

MRA workers were tough. Before the week was finished one of them told me, 'It's no use you staying here, you will just do harm. Until you get honest with your father you cannot play a useful part. Spend tomorrow morning appraising your relationship with your father in the light of absolute honesty, purity, unselfishness and love. Write down all the things that you must put right with him when you go back, and then fly straight home.'

I wrote screeds.

The first night back home I chickened out, I was so scared. The second night, I entered the lounge where Dad was smoking in front of the TV. I found myself saying, 'Do you mind if I turn off the TV because I have some important things I need to share with you; they are so important that I have written them down.' I stood in front of the switched-off TV, read them out in one go, without looking at him once. After a pause he said, 'My God, they did a thorough job on you, lad. It's not all your fault. I've felt you and your mother shut me out. There are things I want to share with you, too.' My Dad became a Methodist Local Preacher, started a youth club and began to share a little of his heart with us.

To my delight, dad, mum, sister and other family came to my ordination on Michaelmas Sunday 1964, in Lichfield Cathedral and celebrated afterwards at a lunch. One year later I was ordained priest.

2

Three Ground-Breaking Assignments

If you feel something, do something.

The Potteries

Ordinands in their last year at theological college have to find a parish where they can serve as a curate and be trained on the job. I was still emotionally unintelligent. I delayed taking initiative in the hope that sooner or later someone else would pick up the tab. I should have appraised dioceses and parishes, identified the type of place, spiritual tradition and parish priest that would best provide what I most needed to learn, and created a network of communication. Despite my inadequacies, God kindly got in on the act.

Among many people whose lives had been changed by Moral Re-Armament were a sprinkling of Church of England parish priests. One of these was Basil Buckland, Rector of St James Parish, Longton, Stoke-on-Trent. A nickname for this city was The Six Towns of The Potteries. Longton was the 'neck end'. It was rock solid working-class industrial English Midlands. (In the 2016 Brexit referendum, which split Britain, Stoke-on-Trent was dubbed the Brexit capital of Britain, since it had the highest vote to leave the European Union.) A significant number of parishioners had never been to London, never mind Brussels. I recall only two professional people in the congregation. People raised their hats when a funeral cortege or the Rector passed by; their hero was Stanley Matthews, the wizard player of Stoke Football Club.

Basil asked me to be his curate, he said, because he wanted someone who had been taught to listen to God. But first, the Bishop of his large diocese of Lichfield had to agree. In those days we were required to address him as 'my lord', and he barked out our surnames.

I did not enjoy Longton. Life was hard for people. Culture was drab. Feuds were normal. 'You've just got to get used to them,' Basil told me, 'they are part of the furniture here'. Worse, the 'churchmanship' (a word afficionados use to describe preferred brands within the church) was neither evangelical (everyone must accept Jesus into their heart) nor catholic (celebrate colourful rituals and sacraments of the universal church). It was merely 'low church' (minimalist).

There was one dead end in this curacy which I shall forever regret. I befriended a teenager in a motorcycle gang. He asked me if I would be their chaplain. Basil required me to say 'no'. A few weeks later that young man, with so much potential, had taken his life. He had been on drugs.

There was yet worse to come. Nowadays, a 'training rector' would be taught how to train a curate and there would be appraisals. Basil did not train me in anything. He did not even allocate duties for the day. Since I had dependency reflexes, this could have ended in disaster, but it did not.

One day Basil informed me why he would not 'mollycoddle' me. He wanted me to be a man, to make my own assessments of what the needs were, to listen to God, and to follow what God put in my heart. 'If you feel something, do something', was his motto. Looking back, I recall three areas of life where I attempted this approach.

The first was with infant baptisms. Most parents who lived in the parish brought their infants to be baptized by the church. Basil baptized them all, after a few remarks, on Sunday afternoons. This scandalized my evangelical feelings. At the very least, I thought, one of the parents needed to invite Jesus into their lives or understand what it meant for their child to follow Jesus. I plucked up courage and told Basil I felt unable to conduct baptisms without providing at least one preparation session for parents. He negotiated this with one family, to my joy. The following week my joy turned to despair. This family complained to the Rector that I had called them all heathens and they would not come to the church again. Following that baptism of fire (excuse the pun), we stumbled on, with me preparing for and conducting a few selectively-chosen baptisms – a typical Anglican compromise!

The second example of this 'God-in-the-heart' approach was when I took over from Basil as Chair of the Longton Bible Society Auxiliary, which raised money for the Society's work of translating and distributing Scriptures world-wide. I sensed that we needed to capture the imagination of supporters with a personalised project for a specific people whom they could pray for and 'own'. So it was that we raised a record sum to buy two thousand Bibles for Kenya's Kalenjin nomads.

The third example was when, after wallowing in self-pity for a year, I dared to listen to the God beyond my navel. The thought that then came, as if from nowhere, was to ask to teach humanities one day a week at the College of Building in Stoke. This was agreed. I did not do brilliantly. Football, sex and motor-bikes seemed to be the only topics that held the students' attention. But I continued to listen. Some Christians linked to Moral Re-Armament were taking a Christian musical to venues around the country. 'Ask the Principal if I can invite this musical to the college', I wrote down in my morning quiet time. The Principal asked me to meet Geoff, the President of the Students Union. Geoff was an atheist. We became friends. He saw the musical, and started the experiment of a quiet time, listening to 'the inner voice'. The musical never came to the college, but Geoff came to God. I was best man at his wedding to Viv in Wales.

Basil may not have been a training whizz-kid, but what he did for me is beyond price. My family stayed with them – something I had hardly dare hope for. They rather liked the Bucklands – Basil, Norah and daughter Mary.

'Build the peace of the world in the streets of London'

My second curacy was in Upper Tooting, south west London, but there were hiccups before it began. Jack Torrens, the Vicar of Holy Trinity, Upper Tooting, another priest with loose MRA associations, had asked that money in a parish fund should be spent on a curate who would develop a ministry to the vast numbers of immigrants settling in the area – a group now known as the Windrush Generation. The Parochial Church Council, however, voted to spend it on a new organ. Jack felt so deeply about this that he called an extra-ordinary meeting of all church members. These voted by a narrow majority to spend the money on a curate.

During this period of negotiation, I was given charge of Saint Jude's, Elephant and Castle, while its vicar had a three-month sabbatical. Noisy lorries delivering goods for Covent Garden market trundled past every night and I found it hard to sleep. I can't think of any member of this small church who was not a Labour Party supporter. It is said that people remember exactly where they were on the day President John F. Kennedy was assassinated. I do. I was in the road outside St Jude's when the church secretary got out of her car and informed me. St Jude's was closed down some years later.

On my arrival at Holy Trinity, Upper Tooting, the church warden and his wife (Jack and Olga – who became friends) informed me that the church did not want a curate and the best thing I could do would be to leave as soon as I could! Vicar Jack had other ideas. He was married to Priscilla and had a son David. He had been trained at Cuddeston Theological College and represented the catholic wing of the Church of England. He believed that to be catholic meant having colour in the rituals and having people of all colours in the congregation. So did I, but it was not easy. Prosperous white people whose contributions helped to sustain my stipend were moving out to greener places, like Epsom. One dear worshipper told me, without rancor, 'I am sorry but I just can't receive Holy Communion next to a black person.' A fine black man named David Pitt stood as the Labour candidate in a general election. He was so unjustly vilified merely on account of his colour that I wrote in the press that 'black is beautiful'. The obscene hate mail this prompted shook me. Jack became ill with it all. However, he had learned to listen to God. During one quiet time God told him, 'Build the peace of the world in the streets of London.' We now had an inspired strategy which would see us through the roadblocks.

I lived in Stapleton Road, by Tooting Bec Underground station, with a landlady called Mrs Watson. When I arrived she said she did not like foreigners and would never have Germans in her house. Before long, however, her front room was bulging with colourful new friends and she proudly boasted, 'This is a proper United Nations!'

I knocked on the doors of people of every type and colour who had come to live in a single room or an apartment. Neither the old Tooting folk nor, it seemed, the *Tooting and Balham Gazette*, had ever heard of them or from them. I enrolled for a course on *How to Write* promoted by the Billy Graham Association. The American course director told us we had to 'get a great idea', ring the editor of our local paper, invite him to lunch and tell him about the great idea. I rang the *Tooting and Balham Gazette* and explained my idea: *Tooting and Balham Gazette* published routine reports of old-time organizations and deaths of local worthies, but its area has become a multi-racial heartland in which thousands of students and others live in single rooms. As a curate I visit these people, listen to their stories, and realize they are like undiscovered gold in our midst. So why not print a story about one of them each week? I would write a column and it would be called *Gold-digger*. The editor never came to lunch but my proposal was accepted and I wrote the weekly column until I moved elsewhere.

The Head Teacher of Tooting Bec Grammar School for Boys asked if I would teach Religious Education two days each week. I replied that I was too busy doing pastoral work. I recalled a cynical secondary school teacher I met on a trip to Egypt who told me his job was 'crowd control'. However, the head teacher would not take no for an answer, and told me that teaching ninety young people would have more influence than having cups of tea with old people! So I began teaching, despite having had no training at a College of Education. It began well, and I enjoyed it. But then three boys in one of my classes got the better of me. They always sat in the back row, made silly remarks and became noisy. I started to shout. The noise levels increased. I feared lest the head teacher would hear the noise and write me off as a failure. Then my sister Sally, who had gained her BEd., gave me a little book on Classroom Management. I developed strategies. Looking back, I realise I most needed a book on classroom psychology. I should have turned their jokes back upon themselves in a friendly way. If one of the boys went badly over the line I should have sent him to the head teacher. I should have shared the problem with teachers in the lunch break and asked for advice. I was too shy. Still, I did try and make friends with these boys.

After that I booked a room at South West London College, which was bulging with Biafran and other African students, for half a day each week, in order to offer personal support. On Sunday evenings we invited students of all races and religions to meet in the vicarage. This included a time of listening to God, the inner voice or conscience. We were careful not to proselytize during those meetings. Once a Hindu who came to these meetings brought a Muslim fellow-student to us during the week. 'He wants you to tell him about Jesus Christ' he informed us. Listening can enable the best form of evangelism. We took parishioners from three continents to an international Christian conference in Switzerland, which aimed to equip people to build God's kingdom on earth together.

Yet there was still a continent inside me which had not yet been opened to God. I developed stomach pain and saw the doctor. He found no medical problem, but told me my stomach was as hard as a cricket ball. I told him it had always been like that. 'Then you should seek help from someone other than a doctor', he told me. But I did not seek help.

I liked our Suffragan Bishop of Kingston, Hugh Montefiore. After three years he invited me over to consider parishes in Southwark Diocese where I might become vicar. By some divine synchronicity, however, the phone rang just after I fixed to see him. It was Noel, from the Bible Society. There was a vacancy for a support worker in East Anglia and he wanted me to apply for it, because he had been impressed by the work I did in Stoke-on-Trent. Initially, I was not interested in a merely fund-raising job, but then I learned that a sea change was taking place in the Bible Society. It had realized that there were not only far away tribes who knew nothing of the Bible, there were emerging sub-cultures in Britain to whom it was foreign. They wanted this new post to engage these sub-cultures with the Bible in creative new ways. I was torn, and shared my dilemma with Hugh Montefiore. He said, 'Ray, God needs some people who have one foot inside the church and one foot outside it. I think you may be one of those persons. If God is calling you to this, I won't say another word about parishes.' I got the Bible Society job.

One foot inside, one foot outside: that characterizes the rest of my life. My passion is Christ seeking to transform the world. For me, ancient church buildings can be but museums, church protocols can be prisoner of cultural ghettoes, and for forty years I have refused to subscribe to the *Church Times*. Why? Because the New Testament forbids us to partake of gossip (2 Timothy 2:16).

Dad and mum

Dad was diagnosed with Hodgkin's disease. He bore it nobly. As he lay on a bed downstairs he said to me, 'I'll have to do something about this'. He died there on 30 March 1968. Among his papers we were surprised but delighted to find a poem he had penned:

> *When I dread each new day's dawning*
> *For the burdens it must bring*
> *Help me to ignore its warning*
> *Simply to Thy cross I cling.*
> *Always, ever lead me onward*
> *With the courage Thy Son gives*
> *To continue through the darkness*
> *Fearless, since my Saviour lives.*

We placed the last line as an epitaph on his tombstone in Aldingbourne churchyard, West Sussex, where both he and mother are now commemorated.

Shortly after our father died, my mother and sister took the offerings made at the funeral to the Tin Hat Pastor's Hostel in London, which took in homeless people. This cause had been dear to our father's heart. In later years I came to realise how much compassion was locked in Dad's heart.

As my ministry in Tooting drew to a close so, out of the blue, did our mother's life. On my day off from the Tooting parish I often went home to visit mum. She was adamant, however, that Sally should take the chance of doing Voluntary Service Overseas in Jamaica. My mother did not tell me she had cancer. In my naivete I wondered why she was widening her dresses. She died unexpectedly during a minor operation. The surgeon said the death was 'mysterious' and there had to be a post-mortem. Yet when I arrived home she had cleared the house and left the deeds box on the top of the stairs. She had inwardly known that she would die, and had not wanted to trouble me She was a tender, loving, faithful mother – a saint indeed.

I had met Sally at the boat that brought her back from Jamaica three weeks previously. Tony joined Sally and me for the funeral. I had no time to grieve. My three years' curacy came to an end as she died. That week was spent clearing mother's house and loading its contents onto a removal van to be deposited in my new house in East Anglia which I had yet to see.

An East Anglia awakening

A week after mum's funeral I hit the ground running in my new job – a packed, pre-arranged schedule of meetings each in a difficult-to-find place, sometimes in fog or ice, in a region I did not know. The Bible Society charged me with turning 116 old fashioned local auxiliaries that raised funds to send Bibles overseas into Action Groups, which combined fund-raising with communication of the Bible to Britain's population. I related to 1326 churches and chapels, and began to engage also with schools, bookshops and prisons. At one level I relished it. I made many acquaintances – but few friends.

The Bible Society provided me with a posh house in an upmarket outskirt of Norwich called Thorpe End. But not for long. A modernizing new management took over. A sign went up at Bible House 'Permanent change is here to stay'. My area was extended to include Norfolk, Suffolk, Cambridgeshire and, for a time, Lincolnshire. I was required to move to a central location in order to save on petrol costs. The society ceased to provide their own houses for staff, but they offered us a low-cost mortgage so that we could buy our own. Without this I would never have been able to own a house later in life. So I moved to Nunsgate, in Thetford, a London overspill town near the Norfolk, Suffolk and Cambridgeshire borders.

My visits to prisons were rewarding. The Bible Society had produced graded learning-to-read packs of Gospel stories. I was allowed to lead learning-to-read lessons based on these. I preached in a different congregation most Sundays. It grieved me that in many villages church and chapel had nothing to do with one another. Even if they were dying, they would mostly die in isolation. If they merged, they would use two hymnbooks, but otherwise remain much the same. The them-and-us mentality reigned supreme.

Although I was mandated to bring change, some people were immune to change, even after the first moon landing. A villager near Ely refused to believe a man had landed on the moon. His friends took him to a house with a TV and showed him pictures of the man on the moon. 'You can't believe that. Nobody's as small as that', he said as he pointed to the figure on the small screen! In contrast, my visits to Cambridge colleges spurred me to present the Bible as something other than a product of prejudice. Don Cupitt, the Anglican priest and Dean of Emmanuel College had launched the 'Sea of Faith'. This allowed him to be an atheist but to value Christian culture. When I told how some South Sea Island pagans had become Jesus followers as a result of hearing the Gospel stories, he denounced such Bible evangelism as mere colonialism and shredded every statement I made. Looking back now I think this was healthy in part, but also immensely sad.

The Bible Society decided to invest money in researching how unchurched tabloid newspaper readers in urban areas might best connect with the Bible. I asked if it might invest in researching how people in rural areas such as the Fens might best connect with the Bible. The Fens needed a fresh approach. The Cambridgeshire and Lincolnshire Fens had the lowest charity giving rate in Britain. The Bishop of Ely stated that many of his Diocese's impressive church buildings had been built as prestige projects of wealthy wool merchants and had never housed a living congregation. I was permitted to spend a meagre four hours a week on research within my existing budget.

Nigel McCulloch, who was then the Norwich Diocesan Missioner and who later became Bishop of Manchester, teamed up with me to visit homes in ten extremely rural parishes in the West Norfolk Fens. We identified that the feudal mentality still held sway, thus removing any sense of initiative among non-landowners. We identified Bible passages, such as the parable of the talents, that spoke to that situation, and we introduced Bible study material to groups in a home or pub in each place.

One perk of working for the Bible Society was that I was free of engagements around Christmas. I therefore took chaplaincies to English-speaking people in Swiss Ski resorts. I fell in love with Zermatt. Upon arrival I realized that everyone I needed to visit was either on the ski slopes or in hospital following a skiing accident. My problem was I did not ski and could not afford the ski school fees. So I approached the Tourist Officer who granted me a week's free ski school pass. I learned there that little children, because they have less acquired fear and are nearer the ground, learn to ski much faster than fearful adults. I also learned that the majority of tombstones in the cemetery are of British people killed on the ski slopes – the British skied before the locals even thought of it. I climbed the Matterhorn as high as you can without ropes. En route I saw a bride and groom emerge from a little chapel with delightful alpine flowers at their feet. This was so beautiful it evoked the hidden artist in me. I descended to Zermatt, purchased paint, paper and brushes, and painted alpine flowers. A picture of the Matterhorn still graces my guest room.

My political and social conscience awakened at this time. I read a book by George Goyder entitled *The Responsible Company*, which proposed that the legal deeds of businesses should require them to benefit employees and the neighbourhood, not just shareholders. Someone told me this was Liberal party policy. I became Chair of Thetford Liberals! As a parish priest and later as a guardian of The Community of Aidan and Hilda I have never espoused a party political view in public – but in this peripatetic role I permitted myself to become active in politics in my home town.

One year before the referendum which voted to join the European Common Market (which later morphed into the European Union) a passion grew in me that electors should understand the soul as well as the economics of Europe. I drafted an unpublished manuscript entitled *The Soul of Europe*. This included chapters on Sergius (Builder of Russia), Wenceslas of Bohemia (Forgiveness in politics) and Birgitta of Sweden (purifying catholic Europe). I organised a coach tour of Europe, which stayed at Taizé in France, Moral Re-Armament's international peace-making centre at Caux, in Switzerland, and Young Christians on the Offensive at Bensheim, Germany.

I was in my element and enjoyed the networking, but my activism hid the void within. Could this be filled? The Bible Society General Secretary, Neville Cryer, stayed with me while on a speaking tour. 'Ray, I sense there is something not right …' Neville drew out of me that I had never grieved for my mother's death. As with so much else, I had repressed feelings and gone through the motions of the new job. I did make a few friends, such as my neighbour and Thetford team priest Paul Oliver. The inner void, however, only began to be filled when I encountered charismatic renewal.

My brother Tony, with whom I had grudgingly shared a bedroom, used to pray aloud in tongues once he became a Pentecostal. In my jaundiced mind as the neglected younger brother, who inherited his clothing cast-offs and lacked his emotional security, this was a form of abuse which invaded my precious space. I vowed I would never speak in tongues. When I accepted an invitation to the Thetford Full Gospel Businessmen's Dinner I kept this vow firmly in mind. However, they did not speak in tongues, they *sang* in tongues –

beautifully. It was like a divine symphony. I loved choral music. I found myself walking out to join them and singing unprompted, unscripted, heavenly notes. I vowed I would only sing in tongues, but after a time I cared not if my tongue singing lapsed into tongue speaking – it was all to God's glory after all! Charismatic people were also involved with healing ministry. One of them prayed for my inner healing. Something awakened, but there was a long way to go.

I collated my findings regarding the Bible and rural regions in a paper, which I delivered to the Evangelical Alliance on behalf of the Bible Society. In this paper I said of certain areas: '… the ground is so hard and the people so pagan, that perhaps nothing less than a community of love in action will suffice to transplant the Body – the Life – of Christ. A community where some work, play, learn, sing in close inter-action with the inhabitants, and which prays and shares freely together.' *Rural Evangelism* was published by the Methodist Church Home Mission Division 1976. Looking back now, I see this as an early intimation of the need for villages of God and a new monasticism.

A friendship grew with Paul Hodgson, pastor of Thetford's Church on the Way. He was keen to meet my brother, since he was a fellow Pentecostal pastor. We took a holiday in Ireland, and I spent some days with my brother and his wife Anita. The talk was entirely about their church and ministry. Something in me cracked. The hurt inner child who felt nobody was interested in him had come all this way to a busman's holiday. This hurt child was starved of love, but his busy public ministry meant he could not admit to this at home. I fled my brother's home and went alone up a mountain. I had never been able to cry as an adult. On that mountain, however, I wept long and loud, pouring out my hurts and longings to God. 'Teach me to love people,' I cried over and over again. A quiet descended after the storm. In this quiet I repeatedly 'heard' an inaudible voice say, 'Accept that you are a pastor'. The following day Paul and I drove homewards towards the ferry. I had the impression that a third person was in the car. It was Jesus. My heart burned within me.

That very week I received a letter from the Bishop of Norwich, Maurice Wood, on behalf of all the leaders of Norfolk's churches: would I become the first minister of a new neighbourhood called Bowthorpe, supported by all the churches? After my 'Accept that you are a pastor' experience, and my call for communities of love at the heart of each area, I could hardly refuse to go for interview.

3

Bowthorpe – a Divine Experiment

This was a dream village until humans moved in.

A town planner

In 1973, Norwich City Council purchased a large area of farmland on its outskirts in order to create Bowthorpe. Experts had advised it that Britain's post-war housing estates were failing. Typically, people from a similar socio-economic background lived in them, problems became endemic, and 'solutions' were 'tacked on' too late. The Development Committee decided to identify the ingredients required for true community. They planned three linked urban villages, each with a village hall, green, school and shop plus a larger shopping area at their hub with health, police and church provision; work and sports areas were around the edges. Cars did not dominate; there was only one (later two) road exits to greater Norwich. Rented, owned and housing association houses (e.g. for students, disabled persons and the elderly) all of equally high architectural quality, mingled in the same street. Eco-friendly cycle and walk ways criss-crossed the high-density housing areas which were dotted with children's play areas and were free from through car traffic. There were nature reserves on the wetlands by the river. The first village centre was put in first – a school, shop, village hall and green, and doctors' surgery. More houses were gradually built outwards from the centre, and then two more linked village centres over several decades. Sadly, by the time the third village of Three Score was built, unredeemed capitalism triumphed and it lacks a village hall, shop and school, though a retirement care village adjoins it. This inspired Master Plan owed much to Bowthorpe's first Project Manager, A. J. Barnard, a former Jesuit.

Prince Charles's book *A Vision of Britain: A Personal View of Architecture* identifies ten marks of a well-built community which 'fulfils humanity on the physical, communal, cultural and spiritual levels': it needs to fit the landscape, be on a human scale with expressions of art and ornamentation, the parts should harmonise with the whole, building materials should be of local character, signage and lights should be unobtrusive, the car should not dominate, high density, community-friendly terraces and mansions are better than tower blocks, building regulations should be used flexibly to serve, not undermine, these principles. I took school children on an audit of Bowthorpe in the light of these ten principles and they gave it 8 out of 10. Residents comprised four out of the five socio-economic groups – all but the super-rich. There was no 'them and us'.

I suppose I was invited to interview because I had worked with all denominations with the Bible Society. Although the Bishop nominated the candidate, because the Church of England contributed the most money to the project, the representatives of the other five denominations could veto the nominee. They allowed me to consult with Ecumenical Projects in England and Wales, and come up with suggestions for an agreeable set-up. I proposed that we would have a leaders team similar to the United Reformed Elders team (the Anglican members of this were deemed, in a legal fiction, to be the Parochial Church Council); an Annual Church Meeting of all members (similar to Baptists), and forms of worship that reflected each denomination and the inspirations of the Bowthorpe church. We were allowed to experiment for two years, after which a sponsoring body appointed by the six denominations would approve or revise.

Several times I took a friend to climb a haystack at what would in a few years be the centre of Bowthorpe, there to do possibility thinking and pray over the land. I did this with Paul Hodgson and John Drake, the charismatic leader of Norwich YMCA, some of whose staff were moving in to Bowthorpe, and I prayer walked the pavements with Mike Lansdell, the Community worker employed by the City Council.

Paul introduced me to a course for pastors created by Jack Hayford of the Los Angeles Church on the Way. It was available on twenty CDs. Until then, there had been a divorce in my mind between Pentecostal gifts and community values. This course taught spiritual formation that was humble, holistic and open to people of all races and backgrounds. The title itself spoke to me: what we were to offer at Bowthorpe was not something to possess, it was a way to be trod.

In a packed village hall during the Week of Prayer for Christian Unity in January 1978 I was commissioned by the Anglicans, Baptists, Catholics, Methodists, Religious Society of Friends (Quakers) and United Reformed churches, accompanied by the Salvation Army Band, with the Pentecostal and Community Church leaders offering the right hand of fellowship, 'to establish one family of Christians for one neighbourhood.' 'I suppose there has never been a service in this country which has been so well represented in the licensing of a minister as this one', said the Bishop. The six denominations would later sign a Shared Church Building Agreement. All but the Catholics and Quakers signed up to becoming a single congregation. After due process (during which I consulted widely) I became a Church of England Vicar, a Recognised and Regarded Methodist Minister, a Minister to Baptists (as distinct from a Baptist Minister), a United Reformed Minister, a Quaker Adherent, and was commissioned to do some initial pastoral visiting on behalf of the East Anglia Catholic Diocese. It was a unique experiment.

What was the strategy for planting a church in a new neighbourhood? The sponsoring denominations were unbelievably incompetent. Most church planters come with a team, a budget, and some resources such as a worship group. I had no team, and not one penny. The first week I printed and distributed a leaflet to every home that announced their church had begun, and asked them to inform me what they would like it to provide. Most parents wanted us to provide a Sunday School. But how could I run a Sunday School while leading an adults worship service? I had to pay for the leaflet out of my meagre stipend. When I made known my need for a float the Bishop's assistant provided me with a £75 float and asked that I repay it within three months!

Yet if I *had* followed that alternative model for church-planting it would not have been truly indigenous. God's idea was that we started as a seed planted at the heart of the half-completed first village of Clover Hill. And the Diocese, to its credit, had grasped this idea in one respect: they purchased an empty shop unit in Clover Hill. I lived above it, and we opened it daily for prayer, newspapers and coffee. We named it The Open Door. The Open Door was opposite the shop, the doctors' surgery and the village hall. We prayed that God would send, or I could recruit, singles and six couples as residents who would be foundation workers. Our prayers were answered. In the first months I personally called on each new resident. Some called on me. Stuart knocked on my door and said 'I've made a mess of life, I think I'll try religion.' He became our church treasurer.

I asked myself what kind of church was meant to grow in Bowthorpe. We certainly had a duty to nourish Christians who transferred their church membership, to be attractive and to make new Christians – but there was something more. Was not God calling us to do in this untrammeled place the kinds of thing Jesus did for three years when he introduced the kingdom of God into Judea? In order to co-operate well with God in this task we had to become sensitive to what was of God in the originating vision of Bowthorpe, for 'where there is no vision the people perish' (Proverbs 18:29 KJV).

Strategic issues had to be resolved. We were to be 'one family of Christians' which meant I eschewed denominational terms such as elders, stewards and parish, but the first strategic issue was whether we were a 'gathered congregation' or a church for the neighbourhood. One brother, who had come from a 'house church', criticized me for spending too much time taking funerals. 'Let the dead bury their own dead' he told me; I should prioritise the building up of a core fellowship of believers. I stood for the idea that we did not have to choose between these two concepts, since the gathered congregation serves Jesus who is 'the man for others'.

Yet there was a chasm between those who thought the church was a preaching house on Sundays with fellowship groups on week-days, and those who thought it was meant to bring God's kingdom on earth, into every aspect of local life. Some of us who believed the latter felt a call to develop workshops or other projects that would demonstrate that God's kingdom was about working life every day of the week. Some of our leaders' team thought that we already had too much on our plate dealing with 'church matters', so all agreed that those who felt called to the new projects should form a separate Community Trust, but that in order to avoid conflict of interest, its trust deed should include the vision of the Ecumenical Project, the ordained team leader should be an ex-officio trustee and the church should appoint a majority of trustees.

Bowthorpe Community Trust turned derelict stables into wood workshops and a shop, sponsored a listening and counselling service which for a time had a room in the Health Centre, and purchased two cottages. One was the home of the workshop manager and the other a house of prayer for a Franciscan Tertiary who offered refuge to battered women or pilgrims. The workshops have had their ups and downs, but are now the UK's chief producers of godly play materials, and Social Services provide placements for people with learning difficulties to work there. A hoped for future project linked to a huge old barn fell through when the barn had to be demolished, but now a separate local charity runs this space as a Community Garden, and another charity sustains the ruins of a church from centuries back as a safe, creative space. Recently a community arts festival was held there.

A second strategic issue was how could we create a unity-in-diversity model of church made up of people of different social backgrounds. Britain still reflects elements of the 'two nations', based on distinctions of class and income. In Bowthorpe the 'two nations' lived in one place. Before I arrived I consulted the Bible Society's skilled church leader, Tom Houston, about how to develop a church that included all classes. He drew a distinction between people who thought nothing was real that was not a diary or agenda item, and those who thought nothing was real if it was not part of a pub jaw-jaw. We tried to embrace both dimensions in one church.

Professional people expected parents to control their unruly infants in church. Non-professionals expected the church to take their kids off their hands when they came to church. Our leaders' team pressed me to lay down three rules for parents. That created a big upset. For a deprived lone parent on medication who could not afford a holiday it seemed like rejection, and it meant they would stop coming to church. I thought the middle way would be for us to create a sound-proof, see-through creche. Instead, we just had a creche!

A third strategic issue was what kind of main Sunday worship service should we have. To begin with, we had the form of service of a different denomination each week, and this satisfied no one. So we set up a working party to study the Acts of the Apostles and our worshippers' views and come up with proposals. The working party concluded that week by week the early Christians had four ingredients when they met for worship: 1) Praise, 2) Word of God, 3) Prayer, 4) Breaking Bread. Ever after we followed these four principles. We often had a Pentecostal flavour to a praise period that could continue for some time, especially as non-professionals often drifted in 'late' in terms of clock-oriented Christians. Yet everyone, including children and former Salvation Army members who have no sacraments, eagerly ended each service in a large circle round the building, to share bread and wine together.

We had an Open Table, which meant I did not refuse to give Communion to Roman Catholics who asked for it, but I did not promote this – we honoured the official position that Roman Catholic mass for Sunday was celebrated on Saturday nights by the Catholic priest whose parish included Bowthorpe. Occasionally I played the piano for this service. One of our leaders' team said: 'Some of us think Christ is on the Table, and others think He is round the Table in the hearts of believers.' Following a visit to the UK of John Wimber, and his modelling of a healing ministry that every church could adopt, we introduced the laying on of hands for healing at our weekly service, immediately after people received Christ afresh with the bread and wine. One day a Roman Catholic member asked for the laying on of hands. He had piles and could not sit down, which meant he would have to cancel a job interview the next day. I laid hands on him and he was healed of piles within the hour. This led me to ask our team why Christians have to war about 'Transubstantiation': if Spirit can heal matter in the case of piles, why can't Spirit transform other elements such as bread and wine? The world church's divisions were not solved overnight (!) but I like to think that we stumbled upon a route to restored catholicity.

A fourth strategic issue was baptism. Some people thought we should baptize every baby we could lay hands on; Baptists and Pentecostals insisted that only born again believers should be baptized, preferably by immersion. We studied the excellent World Council of Churches Report *Baptism, Eucharist and Ministry*, which included the Roman Catholic Church. In this the denominations agreed: a) that there is only one baptism; b) that baptism may be either by immersion or sprinkling of water; c) that, baptism is for believers, who may baptize their whole household including infants; d) that every person who was baptized as a baby and subsequently comes to faith is truly baptized; e) that there should not be indiscriminate baptism of babies whose parents or godparents show no Christian commitment; f) that there must be no re-baptism of people who were baptized as babies and later become believers; g) that renewal of baptismal vows may be in the form of an act of immersion.

We followed these guidelines, even though Britain's Baptists do not follow them, and we did renew their infant baptism in an act of immersion. As they went under the water I made sure I said 'I renew your baptism', even though some told their neighbours they had been baptized! We tried to inspire parents who wanted their baby to be baptized to come to a short discipleship course and to include one church-going godparent. For those parents who refused this, we offered a full-ceremony infant blessing, dedication and signing with the cross (which people called a christening). If they wished they could have godparents and a party. We offered new Christians the choice of baptism by immersion or pouring of water.

Our baptistry was designed by an Anglican architect to be in the centre of the church under the floor. The heating failed for our first baptism. I gave the three candidates the choice of postponing it, but they all went ahead. The first cry that issued from our baptistry was a loud scream from a teenage girl! Other churches asked to use our baptistry rather than the local swimming pool. One baptizand from Norwich Christian Fellowship had converted after being charged for a criminal offence. His last words before he plunged into the water were 'Good-bye'. These immersions became bright stars in the church's year. Adults took videos and children knelt round the edge of the baptistry. I urged Anglicans to build one baptistry for every Archdeaconry.

The tension between members who thought Christians must not waste their time with 'the world outside' and the view that 'nice, liberal Christians never upset anyone' got to me. I became stressed, and was given a month's leave. I went to Post Green Community. I explained to someone that I feared to confront certain church people for fear that they would say this was 'an Anglican take-over'. He said, 'Leadership is not a group of people scrabbling in the mud. Did God call you to this ministry? If so, exercise authority in the name of Christ's call.'

I returned with a new authority and to new allies. A house group had members who I thought reflected the views of three incompatible icons of those days: Ian Paisley (the pope is anti-Christ), Don Cupitt (I believe Christian culture but not in God) and Mother Teresa (everyone is a child of God). Now, Mark Phippen, a grandson of the great Methodist preacher William Sangster, had joined with his wife Barbara. He said, 'We can either stay in the mind-set and jargon of our previous churches, in which case it would be better to return to them, or we can become real and grow as human beings'. We became more real.

We began in The Open Door, but as the congregation grew we transferred to Clover Hill Village Hall for Sunday mornings. Then the first Church Middle School opened at the second village, Chapel Break. I was Chair of Governors. The night before we interviewed candidates for head teacher, the Bible account of how David, the youngest, most unlikely of brothers, was chosen to be the future king came into my head. We chose the youngest candidate, Keith Lilley. He had a wonderful way with children, which in the early years, before the head teacher role required management skills more than children skills, was a joy to see. Keith was a Methodist Local Preacher and I met with him weekly; we often prayed together. Governors and staff tried to be a family, and we had a meal together in a former Manor House once a term. We named the school St Michael's because the ruins of a medieval chapel named St Michael's survived. For some years the church appointed and the school approved a voluntary church worker – the school's preferred name for a chaplain - Liz Cannon. She studied children's spirituality as researched by Rebecca Nye and David Hay of Cambridge University. Few children had a religious upbringing, but when she took them to see trees that had been vandalized, she asked what they thought God felt. 'Gutted', said one boy, 'just like me.'

The congregation began to meet in the school once a month and for a time puppets were used. This raised the issue of whether we continued to meet in a community building, or build our own centre. One reason Norfolk's church leaders chose to have one Christian presence in Bowthorpe was that the master plan earmarked just one plot of land, in the hub shopping centre, for a church. We had to sort out three issues: the principle, the finance, and the place. Some of us felt we would lose our community credibility if we moved from Clover Hill Village Hall. I hoped that we would birth a distinctive congregation in each village, each using an existing building. However, one of our leading voices likened the church to a body that needs its own clothes. The Village Hall had ever-decreasing times when it could be hired midweek: we needed a place where we could manage our own daily and occasional activities. So we decided to build a church.

God surprised us about a third issue: where should it be situated? A Swiss mature student at the local School of Languages, who described himself as 'a community health architect', told me that Bowthorpe residents were 'over-packaged': if Bowthorpe was to flourish at the deepest level it needed a wild space at its heart which could connect people to creation. He described how over centuries European missionaries located a church at the psychic space of each community, which in the early years was a place where nature and spirit drew people. The only wild space left at the heart of

Bowthorpe were the derelict farm buildings and the ruins of a chapel where the previous landowner had kept his pigs. These were opposite the hub shopping centre. We did a survey of residents and asked them to tick whether they preferred the allocated shopping lot or this dilapidated land on its edge for a church building. Unlike our active church members, they voted strongly in favour of the latter. So negotiations began and eventually a new church, with space behind it for a Garden of Remembrance and the site of the ruined chapel beside it was opened. The fund-raising and building management was a major task. We were blessed that one of our members, Robin Manley-Williams, who was a civil servant, reduced to a four-day week and devoted one day a week to this project. The Shared Agreement was signed by the leaders of six denominations in 1986.

Among the many apparently trivial decisions I was asked to make during the design and building process was whether we wanted a clock to be built into the back wall. This triggered something deep in my unconscious. We were not to be slaves of the clock, we were to live in God's natural rhythms. After the first public clock was erected in Cologne in 1370 people stopped listening to their bodies. As Daniel Boorstin wrote, 'Here was man's declaration of independence from the sun ... Only later would it be revealed that he had accomplished this mastery by putting himself under the dominion of a machine with imperious demands all its own'. We created a space at the start of worship during which people could drift in without pressure while a worship band played and sang. I was determined that we relaxed in our natural rhythms with God and jettisoned the tyranny of the time machine.

In time we had a church, the former stables beside it - which became the workshops of Bowthorpe Community Trust - two farm cottages lived in by Trust workers, the gardens, ruins, a new church house of the senior minister, and a prayer cell and saint's sculpture in one complex. Was this a foretaste of an emerging 'Village of God'?

A Muslim student at the Language School opposite told me that he had never seen anyone pray in Bowthorpe. That was because he had never observed anyone make an outward sign of prayer, such as kneeling, during the week-days he studied there, and because he had never heard a communal call to prayer. We took this as a word to us from God. We instituted daily morning and evening prayer, asked a Norwich museum to donate to us an ancient Bowthorpe church bell from centuries back, had this hung in our new building, and tolled it daily at 9.00 a.m. and 7.00 p.m.

Since we had church members and residents with so many different assumptions, we felt we should seek a vision that could be owned widely and grasped at a glance, as commended by the prophet Habakkuk (Habakkuk 2:2). We invited each church group to pray, discuss and suggest phrases. The church leaders went on retreat and decided on 'A heart for Bowthorpe'. This logo was printed on a design of the three villages.

During those early years, increasing numbers invited the Holy Spirit to speak or heal in their church services. Because I stood up front for long periods when I led worship I got back pain. I was told that one leg was slightly shorter than the other, which caused the strain on my spine. A Chorley Wood healing team prayed that my leg would lengthen. It felt as if it did and I had no more back pain for years. At a London gathering John Wimber invited people to come up front who wanted anointing as pastors, then evangelists, apostles and so on. I held back. I most longed to be used like Samuel in the Bible to restore the lost art of listening to our lands. Then he invited those who wanted prayer for the prophetic ministry. I found myself surrounded by a group of ministrants who placed their hands on my ears and prayed long and loud for them. I felt an incredible, seemingly physical sensation. I was convinced my ears were growing ever bigger. I was so embarrassed to be seen with ears like the cartoon character Noddy that I rushed to the corridors where my ears would not be the object of attention. I lingered in a toilet and surveyed my ears in a mirror. They did not look like Noddy's. I compromised, and lingered at the back until I could return home!

We had Catholics, Evangelicals and Liberals – but what about the charismatic and mystical traditions? At the Los Angeles Pentecostal Church on the Way two ministers met in the building on Saturday nights to 'cover' it and the Sunday congregation in prayer. One night the building filled with some kind of golden smoke which reminded them of the Shekinah glory in King Solomon's temple. The next morning, despite the fact that there was no change or advertising, the congregation greatly increased. I and a colleague began to meet on Saturday nights and pray that all that went on in the church worship centre would be aligned with the Divine will so that angels would be in attendance. Shortly after that a worship team from St Andrew's Chorleywood led a week-end. They told us that they felt angels filled the building. I took angels seriously. Despite the fact that there was poverty in the area, I got donations and commissioned a sculpture of Michael, the chief of angels, which was presented to Saint Michael's School.

Norfolk Quakers (the Religious Society of Friends) led Quaker worship in the church every fifth Sunday evening. These became a unique mix of sombre Quakers and chatty charismatics. One evening one of our regulars stood up and said, 'I've had a picture of a ship.' A free-tongued evangelical said, 'A ship is a picture of the church.' 'Oh what a shame,' responded the first speaker, 'the ship has just sunk.'

To their eternal credit the Quakers maintained their solemn silence month after month. Vera was a Quaker who lived in Bowthorpe. One day she informed me in no uncertain terms, 'I am NOT a miserable sinner', as the Church of England's Book of Common Prayer asserts. 'You may not be miserable, but you are a sinner all right', I retorted. Vera thought this was hugely funny and it went the rounds of Norfolk's Quaker houses. On a more serious note, we incorporated the value Quakers place upon silence into our church structure. We had silences after Bible readings in worship services and before church meetings began. Our aim was that our agendas flowed from the silences.

To create an oversight team for one multi-church which serves one socially composite neighbourhood brought big challenges. When we started, the most conservative church people were against the ordination of women. The Church of England required our Church Meeting to vote for or against us having a woman priest if a vacancy occurred where a woman was best candidate. In Bowthorpe's case the Church Meeting vote would also apply to ordained women from other denominations who might seek office at Bowthorpe. Noel, who came from a Plymouth Brethren background, told me: 'I think we need a two hundred year experiment and should then apply the Gamaliel Principle.' This respected Jewish teacher advised that if what certain Christians were doing was wrong it would die out, but if it were of God they should not be opposing it (Acts 5). It was quite a close vote in favour of women leaders.

I myself had unconscious bias. I invited Dorothy Spence, our part-time URC minister for counselling, to chair a church meeting when I was on holiday. When I returned I learned that she had cried while presiding. 'Women are too swayed by emotions to manage a meeting well,' I told myself. It took several years for me to realize that the inability to weep in public is a minus.

During my years at Bowthorpe I was introduced to the Focolare movement, which had ecumenical credentials like ourselves. I joined them in a pilgrimage to Rome. I learned to make inward acts of unity with Jesus in the Scriptures, in the ordained (the foci of unity) and in the poor. My sister Sally also met them. The Focolare (with their unreformed view that a priest's vocation is higher than that of a lay person's) suggested that she lay down her life to help me in my calling. She came to help for two weeks while I had flu, and has stayed in Bowthorpe ever since. Sally took over the top floor of the church house provided for me. She also took the only local job going – the school lollipop lady – until she returned to a teaching post at Norwich City College. Raffaele Zuppardi had been a Verona Father and then married. Following a divorce he had a room in Church House and brought his children to stay with us for weekends.

Nigel Roper heard about the Bowthorpe family of Christians and joined us, since he could not be true to himself in the village and church to which he belonged. He had linked up with the Association of Camps Furthest Out founded by Glenn Clarke. They provided camps where people could become 'Athletes of Christ' who sustain a balance spiritually, mentally and physically, search for God's will; through prayer, respond in love to all people; and seek to build God's kingdom on earth. I gave a talk or two at their camp. Nigel was a footballer and a guitarist and very masculine, so it was a surprise when he plucked up courage to tell me that he was gay, at a time when he thought churches taught that this was a sin. He became unwell. I guessed it was his repression that caused his terrible physical pain. The doctors at first misdiagnosed and then announced he had terminal cancer in his early thirties. We brought him into church house to spend almost his final days. God wrought more deep-ray transformation in Nigel in those few last weeks than in anyone else I have known: our prayer group saw golden rays illuminating his body and soul. His job had not been satisfying but almost his last words were 'I shall shortly begin my heavenly career'. Amazingly, in his last week at Church House he got out of his bed and played and sang with our music group at Holy Communion. I wept as I gave bread and wine with him in the circle.

Ruth Ward could neither read nor drive and her husband mainly stayed at home. She joined our church. She loved the Bible, and found she could read this one book, albeit stumblingly. I remember the first time she read it aloud in church – you could have heard a pin drop. She joined an Adult Literacy Class, and took driving lessons. She passed her tenth driving test! She became a great prayer warrior, a member of the healing ministry team, a pastoral visitor, tended the church gardens, and took people to church in her car. She was a true mother in God.

What began as a dream village threatened to become a nightmare when a crime and drugs wave swept through some of the local youth. This hit the headlines and lowered Bowthorpe's image. I instituted meetings of local professionals – schools, police, social workers, councillors, church workers – and we recognized that we needed to use the media to communicate positive news. I challenged the editor of the *Eastern Daily Press* to print one good Bowthorpe news story for every bad story. News coverage improved. Britain's BBC Songs of Praise usually gathered people from lots of churches in a town to film singing and interviews: we represented all churches so we hogged the whole programme. Our weekly prayer-for-the-neighbourhood group began in silence in order to sense which road they should pray in that week. They sensed they should pray in front of every house in a particular street. Next week the media reported that the drug pushers who paid our young people to pass on drugs lived in the street they had prayed in, and they were arrested. Bowthorpe was part of the struggle to overcome evil with good.

Then, a huge threat to the inspired concept of Bowthorpe hit us out of the blue. The Master Plan envisaged a First School in each Village and a Middle School for all Bowthorpe children. In order to maintain the ratio of church to state schools in Norfolk, this was earmarked to be a church school. Then under Margaret Thatcher's government, market forces displaced social well-being in planning. So we were informed that the County Council had scrapped plans for a Middle School.

A spontaneous uprising the like of which I have never experienced before or since erupted. I was at the heart of it, alongside Dougy Underwood. Protesters lay down in front of buses, and stole numerous headlines. I led delegations to County Hall, our MP, and the Ministry of Education in the Westminster Parliament. The uprising became known as the Bowthorpe Schools Campaign. I have a huge file of press cuttings about it. And in the end, by the skin of our teeth, the decision was reversed. Bowthorpe, as a community, was saved.

We set up a healing and ministry team, and in due course this ministered in streets unsettled by past or present misdeeds as well as in church. In the mid 1500s Robert Kett had led an uprising of soldiers against the Enclosure Laws, which deprived poor people of common grazing lands. Kett's soldiers encamped and fought in the area that was now Bowthorpe. New residents were disturbed by ghosts of Kett's soldiers. We prayed in each unsettled house. One family had poltergeists. Following our prayers this disturbance never recurred. In the second village residents had only just moved into a new street when one young woman shut herself in her car, which she kept in a neighbour's garage, and took her own life. The new residents became hysterical and could not sleep. They called the police, who said they could do nothing, except to call us in. We prayed in each house. We claimed the power of Christ to overcome the powers of fear, darkness and death; we gave each resident a wooden cross to hang above their bed, and invited Jesus to look after each household. This street, too, became peaceful.

One day a prophetic USA speaker stopped in the middle of his talk. 'I have never said this anywhere else', he said, 'but the Lord is saying to you here "Mind the gap"'. He referred to the gap between long-forgotten Christian foundations and our contemporary work to extend God's kingdom. Sometime after that one of our elderly sensitives informed us that she heard monks singing with us in our modern worship centre. Only then did we discover that Bowthorpe had been one of eight chantries of a medieval monastery in Norwich. So we had a glass seat built into the rear wall of our new worship centre, which looks down on foundations of that earlier chantry discovered by the archeologists. It reminds us that we are part of the one Body of Christ that transcends time.

When Toronto Blessing was at its height, I invited a speaker to share his experience with us. I hoped at least one third of the congregation would be 'slain' by the Spirit. However, our leaders team felt the children should be allowed free rein in the main worship area, and I should invite those adults who wanted this ministry to stand in a circle in the back room. As a mere twenty adults stood in a circle I hoped at least one third of them would be slain. No one went down. Until – whoosh – I was flat on the floor unable to move. I just lay there while the entire church's activities continued all around me, well organized without me. The Holy Spirit had wanted the minister to stop being in charge, and many members approved of this experience! One Pentecost Sunday I did invite anyone in the large circle of people receiving Holy Communion to receive laying on of hands for an immersion in the Holy Spirit. A church member recalls me telling people as bodies lay on the floor, 'Don't worry, it's perfectly normal'!

During my eighteen years at Bowthorpe I attended circuit, Baptist Association, and diocesan meetings. I was elected to the Diocesan Synod and the Bishops' Council. But I was impatient with the Church of England. I remember pulsing with a passion for mission when almost an entire diocesan synod was taken up with the subject of cemeteries and bats in belfries. I spoke out of turn. During a Quaker meeting, however, I resolved never again to speak except out of silence. If, during the inner silence, I quaked strongly, then, and only then, should I speak. I never spoke again at a Church of England synod.

Chapter seven of my book *Church of the Isles: The Emerging Church in Britain and Ireland – A Prophetic Strategy for Renewal* (Kevin Mayhew 2003) has a section headed *Bowthorpe – A Divine Accident?* This was the phrase David Edwards, the author of *The Futures of Christianity* (Hodder & Stoughton) and then Dean of Norwich, used to describe this unique coming together of planning and God-guided people.

4

Offshoots from a Village of God

Transformation of the unconscious life of a neighbourhood.

After a decade in Bowthorpe, I was granted a sabbatical leave. I visited the cell of Brother Klaus, Switzerland's patron saint, who is sometimes called the Father of Swiss Democracy. He was a farmer and local magistrate whose family gave him permission to become a hermit. I was drawn to a link between prayer and politics. Carl Jung wrote about Brother's Klaus' vision of the three circles of the Triune God transforming everything: see this link https://carljungdepthpsychologysite.blog/2018/03/03/brother-klaus-by-carl-jung. As I meditated at his cell in Flueli Ranft the remnants of a blacksmith's forge, near my house and our church building, came into my mind. The thought: 'Turn this into a prayer cell for the transformation of the unconscious life of the neighbourhood and dedicate it to Bowthorpe's nearest worker saint, Walstan', flashed through my mind.

In order to respect one or two church members who objected to statues, I agreed that this would be my personal project, it would not be sponsored by the church. The forge was on land purchased by the diocese for a house for the vicar/minister. The diocese told me I could take on this project if I paid for it, but it would mean the house's garden would be somewhat less than the standard size. In the Week of Prayer for Christian Unity the Bishop of King's Lynn dedicated this prayer cell to 'the transformation of the unconscious life of the neighbourhood'.

Some years later, two popular youngsters who were often in trouble with the police, and to whom when they came into the church building we combined friendship with vigilance which resulted in fewer of our products disappearing, got up early, stole a motorbike and went joy riding without helmets. They were found dead beside the road at 5.00 a.m. Their many friends came to the roadside. Where could they gather? They came to the prayer cell, which they called the hut. My sister listened to their memories and feelings, and wrote these down on a large card. For the first time they realized that adults, authorities, church and God were in fact not against them, they were on their side. They held the most unconventional and moving memorial occasion in the church, beside which crosses mark their precious lives. The unconscious life of the neighbourhood had been transformed.

Another offshoot was, in the words of one of our Catholic members, Eldred Willey, 'the decision to invite Saint Walstan back'. Saint Walstan left his Saxon parents' home at the age of twelve to serve God for the rest of his life in the village of Taverham, north-east of Bowthorpe, and was buried at the village of Bawburgh, west of Bowthorpe. There, pilgrims through the ages have come to St Walstan's well. The parish church of our Roman Catholic priest at Costessey was named St Walstan's. We thought it likely that Walstan would sometimes have walked through Bowthorpe. Walstan had outstanding healing gifts with humans and animals. So the decision to dedicate the prayer cell near the Saint Michael workshops and the church grounds to Saint Walstan left its print on the area.

Recently, a generation after I left Bowthorpe, my sister told me that during the isolation of the coronavirus people with disabilities were becoming distraught without their carers. She suggested to one such person that they go to St Walstan's Well, where miracles have taken place, including, reputedly, restoration of sight. 'I think this means restoration of spiritual sight', said the visitor to the well. As a result of the awareness of St Walstan, people are seeing Bowthorpe in a new light – a place where God happenings are on the radar.

Neither the planning nor the Diocesan authorities were aware that the new church building was on the site of a long disused cemetery. Before the first brick was laid, however, the archeologists insisted on a dig, which added to delay and expense. They found out that this was indeed the site of an ancient cemetery (bones had to be re-interred). This proved to be significant in two ways. Young people from the nearby Earlham estate who were up to no good had discovered an ancient map that delineated this cemetery; they took to prowling around and went ghost hunting. Several of them became really frightened. When I informed them of Saint Walstan their focus turned from dark ghosts to saints of light. Rabbi Lionel Blue re-arranged his TV filming of *Holy East Anglia* in order to sit in this cell. He declared, 'Every housing estate needs a saint.'

Halfway through my eighteen years at Bowthorpe, Prime Minister Margaret Thatcher said, 'There is no such thing as society'. Although she actually meant that society is the sum of its parts – individuals, families, churches, voluntary organisations, businesses – for many it heralded the replacement of community with yuppie consumerism. What is the point, I asked myself, of painting the cabin if the whole ship of society is about to sink? I began to search for fresh expressions of the religious life in the market-place. I was encouraged when a member told us on his return to Bowthorpe from Medjugorje: 'It was like walking into a warm womb, and I feel like that about our church, too.' The conviction grew in me in me that trans-denominational faith communities could become building blocks of a new society. This, however, was accompanied by a second, growing frustration. We had taken seriously the mandate to become one, organic family of Christians, but as denominational leaders changed, some seemed to revert to the old denominationalist thinking. In some cases I wondered if all they really wanted was for Bowthorpe to provide statistics that better suited their denominational agenda: twelve more Anglican-only or Baptist-only or Methodist-only members this year. New Christians who joined the 'one, holy, catholic and apostolic church' in Bowthorpe church were more interested in Jesus and the Bible than in denominationalism. They may have been truer to the Creed which all branches of the church adhered to, but they did not tick the boxes on the statistics forms of the regional denominations.

In Bowthorpe we did not ask ourselves, 'What organizational blueprint does each denomination carry?' (that would have led us to hell on earth). We asked ourselves, 'What God-given charism does each denomination carry that we can embrace?' I asked the national moderator of the United Reformed Church if his church carried a God-given charism which we could nurture and he said it did not! Nevertheless, I likened the denominations to church streams. There were sacramental, biblical, contemplative, justice, Pentecostal, liturgical and evangelical streams. We nurtured these streams, or God-given charisms, without being bound to their denominational containers. I asked myself 'Was there ever a time when these streams flowed as one river in this land?' That led me to study the coming of Christianity to Celtic-speaking lands, and to conclude that, despite differences and defects, they did indeed once flow as one river. A hope grew within me that these separated streams, some of which had gone underground, could rise and meet and become one river again.

This led me to start a course on 'Joining the Christian Church'. Years later, Kevin Mayhew published this as *Seeker's Guide to the Christian Church* (2007). In one sense this was an impossible task. Lenny Bruce said 'people are staying away from the church and going back to God'. John O'Donohue wrote that 'in post-modern culture the human mind seems particularly homeless. The traditional shelters no longer offer any shelter. Religion often seems discredited ...' (*Eternal Echoes: Celtic Reflections on our Yearning to Belong*). The Orthodox Church rejects describing itself as a branch of the universal church. However, I pictured Christianity as a tree with three great branches, and a large number of small branches. The tree is Christ's universal Body. The Catholic branch stands for Order starting with the chief of apostles, Peter. The Orthodox branch stands for Relationship starting with the apostle John. The Protestant branch stands for Message starting with the apostle Paul. I likened local churches to banks. Although banks compete with one another, they electronically link up to a vast, single finance set-up. My concern was that if people left Bowthorpe, and indeed while they were members of 'The Christian Church in Bowthorpe', they could join up with a local 'bank' while retaining within themselves the separated strands of Christianity.

Seven years after I arrived in Bowthorpe, Peter Nott had replaced Maurice Wood as Bishop of Norwich. I served on his Bishops' Council. If Maurice was the evangelical Royal Rooster, Peter was the Head of Civil Service. He loved good order, and I suspect would never have sanctioned the experimental basis of Bowthorpe LEP. Good order, however, was accompanied by his need for withdrawal and by a feel for monastic prayer rhythms such as at Taizé, in France. He recognized this streak in me. Near the start of my second decade at Bowthorpe, Peter suggested that I test out whether I might have a monastic vocation. I explored this with Benedictines, Carmelites, and a Jungian-trained spiritual director.

I met with the Minister Provincial of the Anglican Franciscans, and made an Advent Retreat at the Franciscan House of Prayer, at Glasshampton, Somerset in 1987. There, however, my passion focused not on my personal search, but upon the soul of England's national church. Each year *Crockford's Clerical Directory* contained a pungent preface by an anonymous cleric. In the wake of strong media reactions to the 1987 preface, and the unmasking of its author as the Revd Garry Bennett, he took his own life. This hit the headlines as I began my retreat. It was decided no more prefaces would be written. Instead of producing a personal journal, I wrote, 'An Alternative Crockford's Preface'. I printed and sold these and sent copies to fifteen bishops. A magazine called *Prophecy Today* printed as an article the criticisms which formed the first part, but omitted the eight targets for the decade which formed the second part. The eighth target was a renewal of the religious life of the Church of England, which would include a daily worship book for non-bookish people, revival of mission-based Scetes, and a new lay order which linked people who are called to be signs of God's faithfulness in their own locality. This section began: 'The soul of the church is fuelled by its religious life. We are at a moment of Kairos. With sufficient discernment and care, we can lay the foundations for a Religious life ...'.

I then described a vision I had received: A large old oak tree in an apparently shapeless wood was uprooted in a gale. As planners surveyed the scene, wondering with what to replace the oak, an ordinary member of the public noticed that two lines of self-seeded young trees were already shooting up: if they were recognised and given the right management they would make a spacious avenue besides which the single old oak tree paled into lesser significance. I continued in this vein: 'Even as some traditional Orders die, new forms of contemplative apostolates, of hermitages and of monasticism rise up. As these become open to the listening and pilgrimage of their members, and as they dialogue with people in the world's crucibles, they will become instruments of God for our time.'

With reference to the active encouragement of mission-based Scetes linked to Christian shrines, monasteries, retreat centres or churches, I wrote: 'The Scetes of the early desert Fathers, as our own Celtic hermitages, were an alternative to the completely ascetic solitary life and to the completely common life of the highly organised monasteries. They formed a base for mission. At a time when the whole church needs to recover its simplicity and humanity, the establishment of a variety of these is essential.'

Brother Ramon, the Welsh Franciscan hermit who was then Guardian of their House of Prayer at Glasshampton, confirmed the view of the others I had consulted: God was calling me, but not to an enclosed Order. They affirmed my belief in the value of 'the contemplative in the market place', and of what was growing at Bowthorpe. Brother Ramon added: 'You are in the middle of a journey and it is not yet clear how it will turn out.' Something had yet to be born, and it was to do with the vision described in The Alternative Crockford's Preface. As if in confirmation of this, one of several bishops who responded, the Bishop of Edmundsbury, John Dennis, asked: 'Is God calling you to be part of this renewal of religious life?'

In 1996, my final year at Bowthorpe, I was invited to speak at St Ninian's Centre for Evangelism and Renewal in Crieff on the Celtic Way. Peter Neilson, who invited me, was the Church of Scotland's Officer for Evangelism and Renewal. He had visited the ruins of Saint Hilda's foundation at Whitby Abbey. There God spoke to him. Because Hilda's heirs thought the church was about buildings and maintenance, it became a ruin without walls. If her heirs had continued to sustain her original village of God, a church without walls, then even the walls of that abbey would still be there. Peter introduced the Church Without Walls project to the Church of Scotland, which later merged into Fresh Expressions of Church. I saw this as another off-shoot of the villages of God vision, and it had nothing to do with me. Peter and his wife Dorothy became good friends, and then my soul friends.

At Crieff I spoke about the value of communal memory. The prophets of Israel guided their people first of all by reminding them. Moses said to them: 'Remember how Yahweh led you out of Egypt' (Deuteronomy 8). Note the 'you': the people owned the continuity with the forebears who formed their birthright. As living reminders of God's power and compassion, the prophets unmasked the stifling viewpoints of their contemporaries and again disclosed the vision that inspired their forebears and that still offers guidance. Jesus carried forward this principle in his own life and Passover Supper actions. I urged that we must carry it forward too.

A half-way house

Although the Roman Catholics had shared ownership of our church building, and its bishop was a patron of the community workshops, its only official presence was Saturday night mass for Sunday, at which Barbara Fox or I played the piano. However, a number of people who came out of Roman Catholic religious communities found a second home within the mainstream of our family of Christians. In addition to Raffaele Zuppardi, a vivacious lady left fourteen years in a silent Carmelite Order and joined us. Barbara, who lived in the Community Trust's Retreat Cottage, had become a Franciscan Tertiary. At the age of seven she had received a vision that she should become a bride of Christ, but her parents pressed her to work in a solicitor's office in Birmingham. When she retired early to Bowthorpe (she had Norfolk roots) I suggested that she could still honour her seven-year-old's experience and take vows in a Third Order. She did this, sold her new house, and helped the Community Trust buy the old farm cottage near St Michael's Church Ruin, which she turned into a place of prayer and retreat. Seven of us who wondered if we were on a journey towards some kind of lay monastic consecration met fortnightly in my house.

Since I was slightly embarrassed that two former Roman Catholic nuns might be looking to me for guidance, I sought advice from the Bishop of East Anglia, Alan Clarke, who happened also to be the joint Chair of the Anglican/Roman Catholic International Commission. He said, 'I see no reason why you should not draw up a joint rule of life so long as it requires each to be loyal to their own church.' As it turned out each of us, including me, was on a journey that took us in different directions, but that advice proved to be significant. For me it was a half-way house on a divine journey. I drew up a Rule of Life.

During sabbatical visits to pilgrim places I had run out of money. Someone told me I could stay at Marygate Retreat House, on the Holy Island of Lindisfarne at low cost, so I spent a week there. The convergence of history (especially saints Aidan and Cuthbert), nature, and daily prayer in the parish church spoke to me, and I returned each year. As the next chapter describes, a rather messy transition process began.

I stayed eighteen years at Bowthorpe. We had our ups and downs, but overall I loved the people and the place very much, and it is forever in my heart. A picture of the ancient ruin adjoining the new church of Bowthorpe looks down upon me as I lie in bed.

The move had implications for my sister Sally, who was to become homeless. Barbara and Peter, the manager of our workshops, with gracious generosity converted their double garage opposite Church House into a tiny apartment for Sally. I joked that I went to live in a coracle and Sally went to live in a double garage! She has stayed on at Bowthorpe and has been a pillar in God's kingdom there. She is a local saint.

On the evening of Easter Day 1996 I lingered wistfully with two friends, Beryl and Barbara, outside my house following the final evening service, contemplating the arrival of the removal van the following day. I began to doubt. Had I made a huge mistake? I was leaving the most satisfying ministry anyone could imagine for what? Nothing? Then there was a loud cry overhead. 'It's a wild goose,' said Beryl, 'it's flying before you to Lindisfarne.' The wild goose is a Celtic symbol of the Holy Spirit. Like doubting Thomas, who could not believe Christ was risen from the dead unless he was given some physical sign, God had given me a sign when I most needed it.

5

The Birthing of the Community of Aidan and Hilda

This has long-term significance.

In April 2019, three founders, Michael Mitton, Russ Parker and I, spent 30 hours at Gladstone Library, Wales, coordinating our memories of foundational landmarks.

The first landmark for me followed our 1987 Christmas at Bowthorpe when I returned to Holy Island with my friend Stuart Burns. I had decided to return to Lindisfarne at the suggestion of its Vicar, Dennis Bill, in the depths of the winter solstice, when it was dark and damp, visitors were drunk, and the vicar despaired of his empty church. This, we thought, would reveal whether my attraction to Lindisfarne was merely romantic, buttressed by the sunshine of summer visits, or signified a deeper call.

I stayed in a Bed and Breakfast, and was the only one who went to the television room to watch the Archbishop's midnight new year message. This was about the value of cradle places which had brought faith to nations and helped shape civilisation. I guess he was thinking of 'top down' places, such as Canterbury or Rome. I went out alone into the black night and stumbled through the dark into a little prayer cell which had been fashioned out of a stable – a stable, the cradle place for Christ. There I knelt on the cold ground and offered up the island, the nation, and the church to God. Something like an enormous crankshaft turned inside me. There was a shaking, one of those shattering, once-in-a-life-time experiences. I heard an inaudible voice say, 'Canterbury is certainly one cradle, but there is another cradle which is rooted deeper in the soil, deeper in the soul of the people, deeper in the supernatural, a cradle required by the Kairos of our time. This cradle, which Lindisfarne symbolizes but which has been lost sight of, is to be re-discovered; from it there will be a birthing of a New Way in the Church, which has a significance far beyond anything that one person can comprehend. I want my people to re-connect with my presence in creation, in the people of all races and backgrounds outside the church, and within the unseen world of the saints and angels. I want them to get rid of the baggage they have accumulated over the centuries, and to travel light, with room in their hearts for hospitality towards others.' I knew, as surely as I knew anything, that this was from God.

As I pondered this experience it seemed to me that God was calling into being thousands of little Bethlehems rather than seeking to restore one or two Jerusalems. Stuart, the friend who accompanied me on this journey, went back to tell his parish he was leaving to join the new Benedictine Community at Burford. He became the abbot of Mucknell Abbey. I went back asking God to show me what to do with this burden.

A year later Tim Berners-Lee initiated the world wide web. Things would never be the same again.

Following my return from Lindisfarne in 1989, I began to research and write about early Christianity in Celtic lands. I shared something of this vision with Michael Mitton, who was then Director of Anglican Renewal Ministries. He was searching for an authentic model of charismatic renewal that reflected the culture and tradition of the British Isles. He felt that charismatic renewal would run into the ground if it only espoused 'flavour-of-the month celebrations'. He believed that true openness to the leadings and gifts of the Spirit might lead us into deserts of pain and social need, and that it would renew our roots as a people. After reading Bede's Ecclesiastical History, he became excited to realise that the Celtic Church was a model of such a way from within his own land's tradition, and he introduced me to friends who he thought would be interested to do something about this new awareness.

These included his wife Julia, who was working for ARM; Revd Russ Parker, at the time Deputy Director of the Acorn Christian Healing Trust; Revd Carole Parker, Assistant Curate of All Saints Loughborough; and John and Jaquie Peet, unpaid Wardens of Redhill Christian Centre, near Stratford-upon-Avon. Julia was a successful conference organiser, yet recently her spiritual director had told her that she was also a contemplative. Julia wanted to explore how these things could be reconciled, and recognised in Celtic Christianity a way to do this. John had previously worked in the car industry. After he became a Christian, he searched for a church that was as deep but not as overlaid as the Roman Catholic church. He felt that the early Celtic churches were what he was looking for, but they no longer existed, so he started mining and applying the ancient tradition. Russ was a well-known speaker and became Director of the Acorn Healing Trust. He felt that in recent generations God had restored a ministry of healing bodies and then emotions to churches, but that now he wanted churches to heal the land, too. The last time our land was truly healed and endogenous was the time of the Celtic Mission. Russ also felt that he, like so many Christians, had confined Christianity to conventional safety zones. 'But,' he said, 'there is a Celtic wild man inside me waiting to come out.' So the adventure of probing wild and unexplored places with God was to begin.

When I moved to Bowthorpe I sold the Thetford House, paid off the mortgage, and purchased a little cottage as a holiday and future retirement investment in Southe Creake. In 1992, in the spirit of Jeremiah (who purchased a field in the faith that it would be needed when God revived Jerusalem) I purchased with the sale proceeds of the South Creak cottage plus a loan from my sister, the terraced cottage on Lindisfarne named Starbank Cottage, for holiday use. For two years I let this for a nominal rent to Andy Raine of Nether Springs Trust, which was soon to become the Northumbria Community.

Later that year we spent a week at Starbank Cottage (which we later re-named Lindisfarne Retreat) and talked with Nether Springs folk such as Roy Searle. I had a flood of ideas for publishing Celtic liturgies, etc. and possibilities for a presence on Lindisfarne. John

Peet invited Michael to make a retreat with him on Lindisfarne. They wrote down prophetic inspirations including a vision for developing a Rule of Life built on the Celtic tradition.

Michael invited me and five like-minded friends to meet as a group at Red Hill: he and his wife Julia, Russ and Carole Parker, John and Jacqui Peet. There was a convergence of insights in several areas, for example the need to recover elements that once thrived in the early church in Celtic lands, and the need to recover the lost art of listening. A prophecy that Michael wrote down some years later in *A Heart to Listen: Becoming a Listening Person in a Noisy World*, was:

Why do I need people to listen?
Why do I need an army of listeners?
Because my house has been a rebellious house.
The proud speak and speak and feel they have the answers.
The earth is sick because few have listened to it.
The Church is sick because people speak when they should listen.
My poor are sick because people speak about them but will not listen to them.

Why do I need my people to listen?
Because when you listen you meet me in my glory.
You will encounter me in such a way as to transform nations.
You humble yourself to become the meek who inherit the earth.
You relinquish your power.
You let go of what you want to say, and instead,
you wait as you listen, and then you speak to what you hear, and that word will be wisdom.
My world suffers because of lack of wisdom;
wisdom is not gained by talking but by listening.
The fool speaks and plans and fills all silences.
The wise one is prepared to look foolish by remaining silent until they hear a word from the Lord.
Incessant talking has cut my people off from the living word.
When the poor are listened to they start to believe that they are being noticed.

*I am among the poor; you hear my word amongst them,
and then you release my word to the world,
and when my word is released my world will find healing.*

On 8 July 1992 the seven friends met at Red Hill Christian Centre
to reflect and share how this passion for a way of being a church
according to the Celtic tradition was exciting them. This was the
first meeting of the group that eventually birthed CAH. John and
Jaquie told about their Red Hill Project to become a Christian
Centre. Carole felt God was re-calling them to their Jewish and
Celtic roots. Julia felt Celtic Christianity and soul friendship could
be a vehicle through which God could bring about a holy people.
Russ appreciated the Celtic focus on the spontaneity to respond to
the immediacy and presence of God rather than just a conformity
to liturgical routine. Michael was inspired by the way the many
strands of our faith were represented in the Celtic tradition. I
shared my sense of call to live on the island and John prayed that I
would know when to leave Bowthorpe, and when a new ministry
was made ready for me. The six asked me to kneel and prayed over
me in tongues. I had the picture of a boat on a beach with the oars
in place ready to be rowed. Michael suggested this was a coracle
and the place was Lindisfarne. The group agreed to meet quarterly.

On 11 July 1992 I spoke with Hugo de Waal, the Bishop of
Thetford (Norwich Diocese) of a new Celtic Way for the Church
and he had a picture of a shell which burst open and allowed new
life to come out. On St Aidan's Day, 31 August 1992, I journaled:
'I feel called to be part of a training centre here (Lindisfarne)
that has Aidan's qualities ... Steps needed for which I must take
responsibility include: 1) A Rule of Life; 2) A list of those whose
blessing is needed, including bishops and David Adam [Vicar of
Lindisfarne]; 3) a draft training and business plan.

In October the Seven met at Red Hill. After tea we formally
formed 'St Aidan Trust for the healing of the land through men,
women and children who draw inspiration from the Celtic Saints'.
All seven committed to being Trustees. John was elected Chair and
treasurer; Carole – chaplain; I was Secretary and was commissioned
to work on a draft statement of Aims and Objects. Michael wrote

in his journal: 'Our main objective was to get Ray to Lindisfarne to start a work there. It was, we believe, a weekend of great moment.' I wrote in my journal: 'Our rapport is so natural it seems we have been friends for life.'

Anglican nuns had advised the Mittons that if we felt God was calling us not to be a top-down monastic network in the imperial Roman tradition we should call our full-time officer a guardian. A guardian is not a boss, but guards the ethos of the Way. At this meeting I was anointed with oil with a view to becoming Guardian and being set apart in due time to do research and to establish a training centre at Lindisfarne. I had never known what my name, Raymond, meant. On my return to Bowthorpe at 10.00 p.m. two church members, Barbara and Margaret, presented me with a mug they had bought during a day by the seaside which explained that Raymond meant 'Wise Guardian'. C. J. Jung would call this 'synchronicity'. I regarded it as a miracle of confirmation from God.

The inaugural meeting of the St Aidan Trust was held at Redhill on 10 December 1992 at which the Trustees agreed to work together to produce a simple rule of life. At the January 1993 meeting I presented Celtic-style liturgies, which John printed out in the Red Hill office. A charitable account was established, and Wally Hurst from Birkenhead was recruited as solicitor. Early in 1993 there were meetings with the leaders of the Nether Springs Trust (shortly to become Northumbria Community) to share the vision and values of the St Aidan Trust. The meetings were positive, but we decided not to merge. We decided that a Way was more meaningful than a Rule of Life.

The Trust had three goals:

- Restore – the memory and experience of the Celtic Church in ways that relate to God's purposes today.
- Research – this in ways that can help renew us today.
- Resource – people and Churches through provision of worship material, retreats, seminars and conferences – and through an Order with a Way of Life.

We appointed Advisors from different denominations. At the 12 June 1993 meeting Bishop Simon Barrington-Ward agreed to become President. It was decided to invite Stewart and Carol Henderson to be bards to the community. Michael and I were deputed to work on a revised version of the Rule for going public at a Symposium in March 1994 at Swanwick Conference Centre.

This was advertised as Roots for Renewal. At this symposium Michael spoke of the Beatitudes as the basis of the spirituality lived by the Celtic saints and which we need to live by once again. Mark Stibbe spoke of the early Celts as theologians who loved God and lived what they taught. Sister Pamela spoke of the presence of God permeating creation, Russ Parker about healing the land, and I outlined key features of the spirituality that had been lost sight of, and which God calls us to restore. Paul Kyle from Ireland sang and spoke. Commenting on the Celtic-style worship and prayer corners which formed the framework of the symposium, a Roman Catholic from Ireland said: 'This is just what Ireland needs. The Irish people's natural familiarity with God and the saints has been overlaid by second-hand patterns – this can release it again.' Revd Jack Stapleton and his wife Dorie-Ann, had flown three thousand miles from Denver, Colorado, to be at the symposium. Within a few months a US Chapter had started, which we soon regarded as a sister community.

A series of prophetic words were spoken by women, some of whom were weeping for the centuries of belittlement of women in the Church and for joy, for they sensed that God was calling into being a new, creative partnership of trust between male and female, masculine and feminine. It became clear that both our name and our practices needed to reflect the equality and polarity between men and women. Our name needed to recognise people of different races, language and gender, working together for the common good. Although Aidan and Hilda were not universally known, 80 per cent of the worldwide web was in the language they came to speak (English), and because they took an indigenous, not a colonial approach to mission, and were archetypal, they could in time appeal to first, second and third nations of the world. After a period of reflection, we decided to name ourselves The Community of Aidan and Hilda.

One woman 'heard' a rustling of trees. This reminded her of how, when the Philistines threatened to exterminate his people, the God-honouring King David was warned by God not to follow conventional military tactics: instead, when he heard the trees rustling he was to lead his troops from another angle (1 Chronicles 14:15). Was God guiding us to confront the enormous needs of our world from another angle, through the Way of Life God had given to us? We circulated the Way of Life at the symposium, and invited any who wished to follow it with the help of a soul-friend to sign up. Twenty-seven people did so, and I was asked to oversee them.

A portable cabin in the grounds of Red Hill became our office. A Newsletter was launched, worship resource sheets were produced, and people were invited to become 'subscribers' – later they were called 'Friends'. On 21 June 1994 Bishop Simon welcomed us to a half-day at his home. 'Western people are split', he said. 'We need a model of wholeness. We can't go back as if individualisation had never happened, as the Islamic fundamentalists try to do. We must go forward through a repentance and spirituality of the Cross and Resurrection that involves deep listening to our neighbourhoods. I am excited by everything you are doing.'

The First St Aidan Trust Newsletter was published in summer 1994. This, later becoming *The Aidan Way, the Community of Aidan and Hilda Magazine*, has been published quarterly ever since.

From 21-25 July, Julia, Michael, Jo, Chris, and Lucie Mitton, Carole, Russ and Joel Parker, John and Jacquie Peet, Stewart and Carol Henderson and I met for a Caim Council and retreat on Holy Island. On Saturday 23 July we chartered a boat in a direction taken by many a monk from Lindisfarne in order to share in Holy Communion and take our First Vows on Inner Farne Isle, where St Cuthbert spent the last years of his life in prayer, in order to take The First Voyage of the Coracle. A Holy Island fisherman, Richard, took us to the Farnes. Unfortunately, I had not realised that the National Trust who administer Farne Isle refuse entry to everyone who does not come on a licensed boat from Seahouses. 'What if we were ship-wrecked?' we asked the Farne Isle warden. 'We allow people on dinghies, one at a time', he informed us. We went back to sea, and hailed a Dutch holiday cruiser captain. 'If we give you a fiver, will you take us in one by one on dinghies?' we pleaded. He agreed. And his name was Aidan!

One of the children wrote: 'Cuthbert started to serve God when he was a boy. As we sat on the grass we told God we would follow Jesus, like Cuthbert and Aidan did. The birds made a noise all round us, and a boy sat down beside us.' It seemed God was saying, 'Don't forget, I want children to be part of this way.' Russ looked to see if the boy who had joined us was on the outgoing boat. He was not. Was he, then, an angel God had sent to tell us that the community must always be open to children?

At this time the categories of membership developed: Explorer and Voyager (first vows). At the Trustees meeting on 1 August we agreed to form a Caim Council to manage the operation of the community. The word Caim was chosen as a Celtic word representing encircling of the wider community. It was agreed to use the name, the Order of Aidan and Hilda and that I should be Guardian. On a lighter note, the Mitton children buried all of me except my face in sand on Sandham Bay.

My life became like trying to ride two great horses at the same time – Bowthorpe and the Community. Ever more people came to see me to talk about this new movement of the Spirit. Bowthorpe leaders team agreed that I could give one day a week to the Community's work if the Community paid for a one day a week administrative assistant. Maisie Clements was a blessing as Administrator. As the work grew, I raised the possibility that I might remain in Church House as Honorary Team Leader but that my paid post be taken over by someone else. The six Bowthorpe leaders were evenly split on this proposal which hung in the air. My spiritual director and bishops felt I had to be full time, not in two half-posts. To enable this to happen, Bishop Simon persuaded the Church Commissioners' Pension Board to treat me as a monk, offering me a two-thirds pension for life, starting seven years early. In October the Caim Council and the Trustees met together and I shared why I needed to leave Bowthorpe sooner rather than later.

In Autumn 1994 St Aidan Trust Newsletter No. 2 was published with the sub-title, 'Roots from the past for our route to the future'. It included David Adam's Vision of Holy Island in which he concluded: 'Work done by St. Cuthbert's URC, the St Vincent de Paul Camp, The Order of Aidan and Hilda, and the Nethersprings Community have to be all seen as part of the island, and the Church at large'. In the autumn of 1994 a house in Leek was left in trust and was offered to the Acorn Christian Healing Trust. In time this became St Chad's House and for a time was formally connected with the Community. I made known I was willing to commence employment for the Trust as full-time employee Guardian from 1st September 1995. At first some trustees thought I could be employed as St Chad's House warden. Eventually Revds Steve and Sue Goodwin became the wardens before it was handed over to the local Deanery. In November that year I wrote in a circular letter: '... Our difficulty has been to hold at bay the surge of interest while we do the careful groundwork ... I have used every day off and spare moment to write up St Aidan documents, daily 'offices' and resource sheets in the Celtic tradition. It has barely been possible to keep up with a constant flow of inspiration. From Easter our house at Lindisfarne, Starbank Cottage, will be made available to St Aidan aspirants and friends who wish to make retreats on Holy Island; our valued friend Andy Raine will then base his ministry in a place of his own.'

In January 1995 I began my first public engagements for the Community in Jersey. The Caim and trustees recommended that I should give notice from 1 September 1995, if income was forthcoming. I stated that I was willing to work on a faith basis without a guarantee of a full salary. In February I sent a plan for financing my full-time calling to the Caim, and set up a donor and prayer support group that we called Lindisfarne Mustard Seed Project; Russ represented the Caim Council on this. In April 1995 David Adam told me: 'I would like the Community of Aidan and Hilda to come to Holy Island. You have done everything right.' He suggested a property we might buy. In May, Dr Ian Bradley, one of the Community's Advisors, told me he thought a community at Lindisfarne was what was most needed. At that time the Trustees accepted the Caim recommendation for the name to be changed to The Community of Aidan and Hilda, and the magazine to be called *The Aidan Way*.

Jack Stapleton (Guardian of the embryonic St Aidan Trust USA) and his wife Dorie-Ann met at Redhill with the Caim and Trustees. A main focus of this meeting was to explore together the Way of Life. Each shared experiences of healing lands through repentance: Ireland and Britain, Native Americans and settlers; Viking Norway and Britain. It was agreed that CAH groups in other lands should be free to follow their own organizational frameworks.

At this meeting there was a discussion about a community house at Lindisfarne, especially in the light of David Adam's warm welcome. Following a trustees' meeting Bishop Simon sent an appeal letter: 'After much prayer and deliberation over a period of time we have been prompted to move forward to a full-time employee, who we hope will help to establish a community house on Lindisfarne. We wish to invite Revd Ray Simpson to take up this post. We do hope you will give generously to the fund we have set up.'

All was not plain sailing however. I wanted to rush in where angels feared to tread. In 1995 John Peet visited me and informed me that Michael had not been able to apply for a grant for the Lindisfarne house that we had hoped to buy. He and Russ were now questioning the wisdom of buying this property. In July Caim and Trustees met at Bishop Simon's house. The vision for a mission base at Lindisfarne was approved. However, the meeting felt that I should start this ministry on Lindisfarne in Starbank Cottage and see how I could develop office and guest facilities with local support as well as with CAH members. The job description I submitted for myself was approved and the Caim and Trustees joined my sister Sally and I on Lindisfarne, where they agreed to become one group. Children and adults explored various roles in the community. With the Caim and Trustees' endorsement of me being self-financed on Lindisfarne, I launched my appeal for £20,000.

In view of the lack of unanimity among Bowthorpe team leaders, and in view of the anointing and prophetic words about me moving to Lindisfarne I took this as the go-ahead to begin a discernment process with Bowthorpe and Diocesan church leaders about making the transition. I was powered by a passion to seize the tide at the flood. Other trustees had heavy commitments and wanted to go at a slower pace. I lacked the finesse and the emotional intelligence to negotiate this growing gap well. Could I command everyone's confidence that I was, after all, the right person to publicly represent the Community?

The Bishop of Norwich thought I should not have shared my discernment process with our church leaders team. He thought that once a congregation is unsettled, it is too late to change tack. I believed that Jesus wanted us to model trust and transparency and mutual discernment and that I was right to share. The Bishop asked his suffragan Bishop of King's Lynn, David Conner (who became Dean of Windsor) to be my temporary vocations advisor. We could see no red lights telling me to resist a call to be a contemplative in the marketplace and to live in Lindisfarne.

Russ said that I was like the prophet Jeremiah. A fire burned within, and nothing could stop me running with it. Michael, however, was cautious. He was cautious about giving more of his time; he, like others, needed to focus on the demands of his job. He was cautious about money: he had inspired Bishop Simon to endorse an appeal for money for me, but thought we should raise £20,000 before a decision was made about me taking up a new post. And he became increasingly cautious about my lack of smooth diplomacy. Looking back, I guess he realised that I lacked emotional intelligence. In this he was right. For a short period, the embryo community was like two rail carriages on parallel tracks. Michael unscrambled the appeal. I, however, had already begun a discernment process with Bowthorpe, Diocesan and spiritual direction leaders that could not be unscrambled.

A sudden crisis at Bowthorpe brought things to a head. A colleague had to leave quickly together with his wife who headed our administration team, and the church authorities thought that if there was a possibility I would move on, the appointment of a replacement should be left to my successor. It was an impossible work-load. I had to move on.

I was mindful of the founders' view that I should not move until there was £20,000. A farewell and launch of my first full length book *Exploring Celtic Spirituality* brought in £11,000. Lindisfarne Mustard Seed Project supporters held car boot sales and coffee mornings at Bowthorpe, the Bishop most generously 'managed' Church of England legalities to enable me to have three months stipend by making me a curate for three months on the day I left the Diocese! And I made a business plan to use my spare room as a B&B. Together this seemed to me to ensure the amount the founders had required before I moved, so I agreed with the church authorities that I would tender my resignation in 1996.

However, in September the Caim and trustees asked me to delay my departure from Bowthorpe until the full amount of cash was in the bank. But back in Bowthorpe, an understanding had been reached by all the six participating denominations in the Local Ecumenical Project that my departure would be sooner. So, in October the Caim and Trustees resolved to release me to pursue my calling independently of the community of Aidan and Hilda. We all agreed to surrender our roles for a season of prayer and waiting on God. Michael and Bishop Simon sent a circular letter which stated '…(The situation at Bowthorpe) has put pressure on Ray to move sooner rather than later, and everyone recognizes that the fire in him burns strongly; at the same time the Caim Council increasingly felt it was not ready to take on such a major organisational burden. At the Caim Council of 10 October there was unanimous agreement that the right course of action was to release Ray to pursue his own ministry at Lindisfarne, and to seek to establish a house of prayer there, thus freeing Ray from the restraints of the Community's formal structures. Though he will retain close links of prayer and fellowship with the community and remains on the Caim Council. We hope that you will feel that any money you have given can be used to support this new ministry … We believe this is the Celtic way … to push out in small coracles.'

By February 1996 Lindisfarne Mustard Seed Project (LMSP) was established as a registered charity. Steve Dale, a colleague from Bowthorpe, was its Chair. Its purpose was to fund my ministry and any centre on Holy Island.

The truth is I arrived on Holy Island with a feeling of desolation. I would have done well to recall words I wrote to Michael on 17 November 1993: 'John Finney's perceptive advice not to purchase property set my mind towards sailing off in the coracle with all the grief that brings … John Peet sensed that if Redhill is to become a sign of this new way, people concerned will first have to go into the desert. Carole seems to think this way too. So we are desert travelers together. Let us pray for one another in this light …' A year or two after this I received a hand scribbled post card from Bishop Simon, now well retired in Cambridge, in which he wrote that he rejoiced at everything he heard about the Community of Aidan and Hilda, was sure my ministry was borne of the Holy Spirit, and he repented of his part in what had happened.

The chaplain of a Healing Centre stayed long in prayer in the upper prayer room of Starbank Cottage. He had a prophetic picture of an aborted baby. I understood that this aborted baby was either myself or the embryo Community of Aidan and Hilda. Then, however, as he continued in prayer, he noticed that the baby was alive after all. In my destitute state I realised, that even if no human being could see what was in me, God's nature and name is 'Thou, God, seest me' – He knew what was in me. I must go back to my Community of Aidan and Hilda family.

I met with the gaitered Bishop of Newcastle, Alec Graham, who gave me permission to officiate in churches in his diocese. En route to this meeting I called on George Bebawi, a Coptic theologian. He said, 'Ask the Bishop if he will turn his Diocesan offices into a Spirituality Centre; every Diocese needs a spirituality centre'. Alas, it seemed to me that the spirituality of the Diocese then was far from that vision. The Bishop spent not thirty, but the entire forty-five minutes talking about canon law. I went out into the streets of Newcastle and wept for its people who seemed like sheep without a shepherd.

In 1996 invitations flowed in for me to talk about CAH throughout the UK and Ireland, including Jersey (again), Glastonbury, Glasgow, York, Whitby, and Whithorn. Michael saw me at a conference and said 'I see the Holy Spirit is in you'. In July of that year members of the Caim and Trustees had a sense that this was the time for members to resume their former roles, which included recognising me as the Guardian of the Community.

Retreatants to Starbank Cottage spent time in the upstairs chapel that I created. People had significant encounters with God. Two in particular from Norway, Andreas and Siri Kratzmeier, would return to help set up The Open Gate. In October 1997 John Peet asked that the CAH office be transferred from Redhill to Lindisfarne. Charlotte Lobb was employed as part-time secretary.

On 10 May 1998 CA&H Trustees published Roles, Responsibilities and Relationships of Trustees, Caim Council and Guardian. At this time the Caim membership was changing. Its chair became Revd Gordon McGuiness. Its Treasurer was Revd Mark Slater and I was the Secretary. Father Cliff Bowman and Sue Clarke also became members. It met at Luton, Nottingham and Lindisfarne. Following the retirement of Bishop Simon, Ian Harland, Bishop of Carlisle, was appointed as Community Soul Friend.

That summer John Peet was diagnosed with cancer, which proved to be terminal. On 3 May 1999 he died. Russ and Michael officiated at the funeral and at the burial I placed his CAH cross in his grave while we all sang 'Let the saints go marching on'. Michael writes about John and Jacqui on pp. 140-143 of his book *Wild Beasts and Angels* (DLT). Jacqui was a co-warden but was required by Red Hill trustees to leave and subsequently, with much sadness, severed links with Red Hill and ceased her CAH involvement. At the Annual Gathering at Red Hill, I identified four foundational gifts with which John had blessed the Community: 1) His hunger for a new way of being church; 2) A commitment to reflect the spirit of the monasteries in the God-centred simplicity of everyday life; 3) Prophetic words about listening and restoring and weaving that became incorporated into our Way of Life; 4) A model of hospitality that John and Jacquie offered together so authentically.

Around this time Russ stepped down as a Trustee, but retained his support of the Goodwins for five years. At this time Stewart and Carol Henderson, Carole Parker and Julia Mitton also stood down. Michael Mitton, having become Deputy Director of Acorn Christian Healing Foundation, in charge of its Christian Listeners' programmes, continued for a period to be a trustee until other trustees were in place, and then resigned. I was therefore the only one of the seven co-founders who continued to exercise a leadership role in the community, although Russ and Michael continued their close association with the community and have led retreats.

The newly staffed Caim Council organized a national annual gathering, and a January annual retreat followed by a business meeting for Voyagers. At one of these a prophetic Baptist minister named Sean Blackman prayed over me. As Moses' work-load increased and he came to the limits of his abilities, God told him to appoint Aaron and Hur as his right hand and left hand helpers. I needed to do the same. So after due process Simon Reed and Graham Booth became deputy guardians. Simon was a West London Vicar; Graham was by then engaged in full-time work for the Community on Lindisfarne. Both these remarkable leaders have God experiences about which a book could be written. A year or two later Sean again prayed over me. Moses also appointed a younger person to carry the work forward into the next generation – I needed to appoint a Joshua. So David Cole became our Explorer Guide and young people's worker. He is now our first monk-in-habit Voyager and our Deputy Guardian. He has flowered into a great author and connector.

Many signs of Providence took place on Lindisfarne and in the ministry of some dispersed members. The Community took root in Africa, Australia, Canada, Denmark, New Zealand and Norway. Members included Catholics, Orthodox, Episcopal, Reformed and Independent Christians, plus a few agnostics or former pagans who wished to journey further, starting where they were.

A website was launched, managed by Paul Swinhoe, building on the first in-house website established at The Open Gate by Daniel Hug. Area groups were formed. Regional soul friend advisors were appointed. A quarterly prayer diary was sent out with the magazines. Resources were regularly published. A Handbook was compiled which outlined prayers, principles, structures and personnel of the dispersed Community.

Martin Warren, a Devon priest, started to lead CAH pilgrimages. Retreats were held. We established a link with the Sisters of the

Holy Paraclete at Whitby and held an annual St Hilda's-tide retreat at their St Oswald's Pastoral Centre. At one of these, three members by chance had rooms in one bungalow a stone's throw from the main retreat house. They were Penny Warren, Graham Booth and Simon Reed. After a 10 p.m. cuppa they felt an impulse to go aside to a room to pray together. They finished praying at 2.30 a.m. A divine bond was formed that would bear much fruit.

In 2010 I reached my seventieth birthday, and announced that I intended to hand over the guardianship. Over the coming months discussions took place. It was thought that we should have more than one guardian, and ideally male and female. Voyagers were invited to propose, vote for and endorse names.

In January 2011 I flew from Australia to our Voyagers Retreat at Worth Abbey, Devon, and handed over as UK Guardian to three part-time guardians: Graham Booth, Simon Reed, and Penny Warren. This was a formative moment in the Community's DNA: they were not only an expression of male and female partnership, they were an expression of the Holy Trinity – and they had been brought together by a sovereign move of God before they were elected. Penny became the Members' Guardian, and we have realized ever since the invaluable presence she has brought to the leadership. She was born to this vocation. I had appointed only males. God had in mind a contemporary Mother Hilda who would, like her, be a jewel.

Power tends to corrupt said John Acton. Shortly after I handed over, a bishop told me that every Anglican community had experienced power struggles when its founder gave way to a successor. We seemed so joyful, he said – what was the secret? I told him that the secret was to work through those issues before rather than after the handover. We were committed to do constant work on our own false egos. But with the best will in the world we can remain blind to aspects of our ego. We can hang on too long, and fail to risk a younger person flowering or floundering when they are given full responsibility. We had already changed the constitution so that every five years a guardian was required to stand down or seek re-endorsement by a vote of members. I had already said I would stand down when my current five years expired, but as a result of a challenge I agreed to hand over eighteen months earlier than this.

Almost the last thing I did before handing over as guardian of the Community was to finalise the process whereby it became, among other things, an Acknowledged Anglican Community. We had always sought to find the best way of relating to each 'branch' of the universal Christian Church. Now that the Church of England Advisory Council for Relations between Bishops and Religious Communities had recognized a new category – a community which consisted of members of different parts of the universal Body of Christ, but which included an Anglican Episcopal Visitor among its different referees – we signed up to this.

Someone jokingly pictured Graham as Abbot, Simon as Bishop and Penny as Spiritual Formation Guardian! In an act of affirming and freeing kindness they decided that I should be known as The Founding Guardian. I no longer had any control over decision-making, but through relationships, networking, prayer and writing I could continue to input into the foundations of our world-wide family.

Six months before that, however, on 27 July 2010, I hired an educational charity's boat, and Simon Reed and I became the first CAH members to take life vows. We took the Long Voyage on a London river. Our vows were witnessed by Rachel Treweek, who shortly after became the Church of England's first female Diocesan Bishop. Among our guests were my cousin Father Ken and my publisher Kevin Mayhew, who renewed an ancient friendship. Simon and I had to duck every so often to avoid our heads hitting a bridge. In between bridges we each pledged: 'I put my hand to Christ's plough. I will not look back. I will set sail in Christ's ocean. I will go where His Spirit leads … I belong to Christ and commit to this calling now and forever … I undertake to live by this Way of Life without reservation, and to be a faithful member of the Community of Aidan and Hilda for the rest of my life, God being my helper.' Was this voyage and the bridges a parable of the Community? We have to duck and weave through the slings and arrows of outrageous fortune, but there can be no doubt about God, our life vows and the Way of everlasting Life.

6

Lindisfarne – a Holy Island?

Ebb tide, full-tide, how life's beat must go.

The Holy Island of Lindisfarne vies with Iona to be Britain's most significant holy island. It is a thin place. Pilgrims from around the world find God here; they are changed by the special quality of the light, the dunes, the singing seals, the shores, its saints and the centuries of daily prayer continued to this day. Legend says that the devil fought with the archangel Michael, and threw his axe into the north sea which became Lindisfarne. The island is the shape of an axe head – the causeway is like the long axe handle. Lindisfarne was the monastic base of Saint Aidan's seventh-century Irish mission to the English. From its Scriptorium came the magnificent Lindisfarne Gospels, which *The Sunday Times* described as 'the Book that made Britain'.

It is a tidal island on Britain's north-east coast, some fifteen miles south of England's border with Scotland. It has a fractured history. The Celtic name for the island was Medcaut, meaning place of healing. The indigenous Celtic peoples laid siege to invading Anglo-Saxons who gathered their forces on the island in the sixth century, but they quarrelled among themselves and allowed the Saxons to take over. The island of healing became the island of disappointment and lost hopes.

For a generation, under Aidan, the Irish monk sent from Saint Columba's monastery on Iona, it became a loved mission base with the favour of the people and King Oswald upon it. The brothers walked among the people, were loved by the poor, and bought slaves their freedom. Lindisfarne housed probably the first monastic school for English boys outside Canterbury and was a place of holiness and hospitality. But after the 664 Synod of Whitby all the Irish brothers and thirty English monks fled to Ireland: they could not bear to live under the new Roman regulations. Those who remained groaned under the new regime. It was not a happy place. Prior Cuthbert helped them to accept the inevitable and to mellow; he prayed at night on what is now known as St Cuthbert's Isle. It again grew large, and prestigious, and its scriptorium produced the famous Gospels. Saint Cuthbert, whose body did not decompose, was enshrined there and the island became Britain's largest pilgrimage centre. A king of England decreed that Lindisfarne should be known as Holy Island. But that period also ended in tragedy. The island became the first place in Britain that the Vikings ransacked. In 795 monks were taken captive, the rest fled, and eventually laid Cuthbert's body to rest at Durham.

A few centuries later the Durham Benedictines, who guarded the shrine of St Cuthbert, built a daughter priory on Lindisfarne. By most accounts the monks, who reflected Britain's new feudal class system, were never loved as Aidan's monks had been. At the dissolution of the monasteries between 1536-1540 islanders built their own homes with stones from the priory.

Because the island is tidal it is cut off from the mainland when the tide is up and joined to the mainland when the tide is low. With the coming of the motor car and the building of a small bridge crowds began to come, and they have been coming ever since.

I have described my annual visits to the island, my encounter with God at midnight on New Year's Eve, and my call to become a founder of a new monastic community. Before I decided to live on Holy Island I put out a fleece. I would only come if its vicar, David Adam, welcomed such a move. This was in line with Jesus' teaching that his disciples should only go where they are welcomed. David explained that he had dreamed of starting an SAS (the name of the UK's front-line Special Air Service whose motto is 'Who Dares Wins' – Churchill was referring to these fighter pilots in his famous World War II speech 'Never in the history of mankind have so many owed so much to so few'), but for David these initials stood for Saint Aidan Society. He had never got round to starting this himself, so he would welcome a Community of Aidan and Hilda presence on the island. Indeed, David had a vision for Holy Island to become a spiritual hub for northern England. In a 1994 St Aidan Trust Newsletter (which shortly became the CAH magazine *The Aidan Way*) he outlined this vision:

> I believe that this is a vision for the church at large but earthed in a particular place. I also believe we have the resources for mission, even the vision but we do not often have the personal motivation. I have looked at vision in four directions, which put together make the shape of the cross.
>
> The Downward Reach: I see the church on Lindisfarne as being Celtic in its view of a very present God. I would like the church to be a place where we celebrate the Presence, where we proclaim God is here. So I want the church to be seen as a TOUCHING PLACE, where heaven and earth meet; a truly incarnational church. To encourage folk to see that God is here – and with them … It means being a TEACHING PLACE, where schools, groups, pilgrims and tourists can all come and have some input. It will be also a place for retreats, spiritual renewal, courses and day experiences. Again this will demand some staffing… I would like to see a TRYSTING PLACE, where people took part in some form of dedication and accept a simple Rule of Life.
>
> The Upward Lift: We need to be a place that proclaims the resurrection and ascension – and more – the presence of the Risen Lord. Though God is in our midst, we need to let people also experience the God beyond. We seek to be an EXTENDING PLACE, to show that our faith extends our life and our horizons rather than restricts them. To be a place that encourages people to look beyond, a place of prophecy and vision. We need to be an ELEVATING PLACE that is able to uphold those that are down … Many people coming looking for help, attention, a listening ear, all wanting uplifting …The liturgy needs to speak instantly to the visitor who does not come to church very often – here the use of Celtic style prayers can be of great use.

The Inward Pull: The church ... needs to be open armed, and open-minded – many prodigals come here from a far country. There should be someone to listen to them and make them welcome. We need an ACCEPTING CHURCH, where we can provide a counsellor, a confessor, a comforter and a Soul Friend to all who come in need. We need to be an AFFIRMING CHURCH that declares and shows the love of God for all his creation. We need to see Christ in others and to be Christ to others. We need to be a place where people are drawn to the very sanctity of the place.

The Outward Thrust: In the style of the early Celtic church, we need to be a SENDING CHURCH, encouraging people to share their faith. Training people to go out to proclaim the Good News. Of such people and others we need to be a SUPPORTING CHURCH meeting their needs and helping them to find answers to the questions they ask. Finally we need to be a STRENGTHENING CHURCH through the power of the Spirit. A place where people can come for refreshment and renewal.

Because we are talking of the Church and not a single denomination. I would like to see this being achieved ecumenically and not just by a single group (as if that were possible). Such a vision must also include Marygate House and its work with courses and retreats. It must look at any other groups that seek to be linked to the Island and see where we can work together. Work done by St Cuthbert's URC, the St Vincent de Paul Camp, the Community of Aidan and Hilda and the Northumbria Community have to all be seen as part of the Island and the Church at large.

For those who live on the island their natural surroundings are second nature. Fishing, farming and catering for tourists are hard work. Their history is replete with hardship and pains. The island consists of islanders – those who had a grandparent living on it – and incomers. Alastair McIntosh, who lived on a Hebridean island for thirty years, wrote in his book *Soil and Soul: People Versus Corporate Power* that incomers are disliked for their first decade, tolerated for their second decade, and if they are lucky, they are adopted in their third decade. I hoped I would be lucky, and indeed I think I was adopted by some islanders, but a minority wanted rid of me. It broke my heart.

There are two sides to every story. Mine is one side of a story. Screwtape's is another. Almost any resident or institution you ask will tell another side. God does not take sides. But I will tell you a little of my side of the story.

I was drawn to Holy Island because it was removed from the mad rush of commercialized places, it was a place of nature, history, daily church prayer, of connection with St Aidan, and some pilgrims who were drawn to Lindisfarne were also drawn to a spirituality such as we offered. A therapist and spiritual director of great insight confirmed that there was such synchronicity between myself and Lindisfarne that I should go for it. The other community founders believed that, when the time was right, I was meant to live there. That is why, when David Adam welcomed me, I decided to live there. None of this, however, was known on the island. I went seeking to be anonymous: with hindsight, I should have introduced myself to each group and pub, especially as one islander scoured the Community's new website, with its mission statement that 'the whole created world may be reconciled to God through Christ', and concluded we were a threat.

I have described how I was able to secure Starbank Cottage as a holiday base. I moved into it although it had no garden and little privacy – you could see into the upstairs bedroom from the semi-public lounge below. In order to survive financially and model hospitality and prayer from the start, I turned the smallest downstairs room into a guest B&B room, and half the upstairs into a chapel where daily prayer rhythms were observed. I put in a partition and slept behind that. I could no longer afford even newspapers or haircuts. People began to stay. One was so touched by his experience that he became an Explorer and then an Orthodox Christian. Another couple heeded a call to emigrate to Norway following a week's retreat. Andreas Kratzmeier, upon learning how skint I was, prayed 'Oh Lord, may Ray sell more of his books tomorrow than he has ever sold before'. That is exactly what happened: one order came from an island shop, and two other orders followed the same day!

Shortly after my arrival the strange sound of singing seals filled my ears. 'Are they in childbirth?' I asked David Adam. 'No, they are praising God', he replied. Julia Mitton had encouraged me not to go to Holy Island with a blueprint, but to go to St Cuthbert's Isle under a full moon and become completely still. When I learned to do that, she suggested, all would unfold. In due course I did just that. I dedicated a year to listening to the island and to pilgrims. I recognised that the rhythms of the tides were important to the fishermen and to all islanders. As I listened to pilgrims I became aware of a substantial number who came spiritually thirsting. They wanted someone to listen to them or they hoped to find a lived spirituality somewhere on the island that they could dip into. Above all, a longing grew in me that pilgrims and residents might connect once again with the humble dynamic of gentle Aidan, who walked among the people and imposed nothing alien.

So, the following year I arranged four retreats, using local hotels or Marygate House, which allowed groups one booking each year. These retreats were valuable, but it was hard to create a communal spirit when there were competing meal times and other noisy guests. At the close of a retreat on soul-friendship I asked retreatants to pray that we might be able to have our own retreat house. A few days later Tania Witter phoned from London: they let out an apartment for income; would we like them to sell this, buy the guest house that was currently for sale on Holy Island, let it to us for a moderate monthly rent, and give us four years to raise the funds to buy it? This seemed like answered prayer, so we said yes, please, but would they let us pay rent in arrears because we had no money!

The sale to the Witters was not completed until July 1998. The season was well advanced. We needed to hit the ground running or else we would miss the season and the income needed to pay our rent – and we had to buy furniture and cutlery. As if by a miracle Andreas and Siri Kratzmeier came from Norway to get us launched. Andreas went to Alnwick auctions and furnished us quickly at bargain prices. We opened throughout August and were able to pay our first rent on time. Andreas is a brilliant entrepreneur and physically strong. He found a large Norwegian railway sleeper washed up near the bay where the Vikings landed in 793. He heaved this to the end of a track and helped me place it in my car. He cut it into two and fashioned it into a large cross. This has been a focus of our prayer room ever since – a reminder of our calling to heal wounded memory.

The property was known to Islanders as North View, although the sea view had long been obscured. They said it was the island's oldest building, and stone from the Benedictine priory had been used to build the wall around the fire place. David Adam's book, *The Open Gate,* was sold in the Post Office, and explained the value of an Open Gate in Celtic folk lore – it represented possibilities to explore fresh horizons. We decided to call the retreat house The Open Gate, but in order to honour island memory, our large sign featured it as The Open Gate at North View.

We sought to respect and fit in to the rhythms of the island and the local churches. For example, we supported the two morning and one evening daily services at St Mary's Church, arranging meals and programmes so as not to clash with them. We offered the Community's midday and night patterns of prayer in our downstairs cellar 'chapel'.

We wrote in to the job description of our warden the need to respect the way of life and rhythms of the island. We linked over-flow guests with island B&Bs and encouraged guests to buy food and gifts on the island.

My friend and colleague Canon Kate Tristram, who during our first years was warden of Marygate House, a retreat house owned by an independent Christian trust that a previous vicar had started, likened Marygate House to a bumblebee. According to the laws of science, it should not be able to fly, but it does. She outlined the catalogue of impossible difficulties that Marygate House had encountered. According to the usual norms it should have closed down, but the providence of God had kept it 'flying'. Our experience at The Open Gate was in some ways similar. Its story, too, is like that of a bumblebee. Retreat House wardens do not grow on trees. Hardly one person in a million could possess the practical, management, inter-personal and spiritual skills, the energy levels, dedication, and vocation to live by our way of life and relate well to the island with just an honorarium, not a proper salary. Yet despite failings, God has always worked in the lives of Open Gate guests, under every warden. If I had written their stories down they would fill volumes.

Before I went to university I reached grade 7 in pianoforte, and loved tinkering on my piano throughout my first four postings. However, there was no room for a piano when I had to downsize in order to come to Holy Island. So I gave my piano to a friend and my music to a charity shop. A few years after I arrived on Holy Island St Mary's organist, my friend Beryl, suddenly died of a heart attack. There was no one to play the organ and I was asked if I would play. 'I can't play the foot pedals,' I explained. 'That doesn't matter,' the vicar explained. So I became the unofficial organist. I ordered a booklet from the Royal School of Church Music entitled *The Reluctant Organist*. It urged me to be content with simple tunes. So I played Taizé chants. Then I read *The Inner Game of Music*. It advised me not focus on technicalities but to abandon myself to the spirit of the music. I purchased secondhand copies of organ music. One day the queue of people waiting to receive Holy Communion was extra-long. I had no more music in front me. I thought to myself, 'I can sing in tongues – could I play music in tongues?' I let my fingers follow the music that was present that moment in my soul. After the service the vicar asked me, 'What music was that? It was beautiful.'

At Bowthorpe I worked with all denominations and the Community's Way of Life called us to weave together the different strands of Christianity, so I intentionally avoided getting so involved in the Church of England's Newcastle Diocese that it compromised this bigger calling. The world was my parish. I cast our bread upon the waters rather than restrict energy flow to just one canal. I think I did the right thing, but this had consequences. Perhaps some people felt I did not conform to 'the system' they took for granted.

Ian Fosten, who was then the Director of the United Reformed Church's St Cuthbert's Centre, asked me to lead the Saturday night service there that fell on Halloween. I was minded to identify and dispel any dark, destructive spirits on the island. David Adam cautioned against this. 'Don't stir them up and give them a prominence they don't deserve,' he advised, 'celebrate all the saints and they will fade into the background.'

We had a series of wardens – Ross and Jean Peart were followed by Clare Short. Each had ups and downs but genuinely sought to offer gracious hospitality, and throughout there was a steady stream of miracles in the lives of guests from many lands.

Tom Martin Berntsen, a sailor and pastor from Norway, sailed over on a pilgrimage. He had long felt that committed Christianity in Norway must mean more than just attending church services. He spent a night in prayer on Lindisfarne's St Cuthbert's islet. 'God has told me to invite you to a lighthouse in Norway,' he told me next morning. 'God has not told me', I replied. When I learned that Norway's lighthouses are now B&B's I changed my mind! So I spent two days with his prayer group (which included the Chief of Police) in a Bed and Breakfast former lighthouse. The Community of Aidan and Hilda (using also the name Anamcara) was soon launched in Norway.

A man came from the Netherlands. He explained that he was not religious, but he had come to see the Lindisfarne Gospels. He spent hours gazing at the digital version in the Lindisfarne Centre two doors down. He then spent hours in tears, in our chapel. Eventually he asked if I would bless his wedding ring.

From Australia came Brent Lyons Lee. He was torn between the evangelistic approach in his two days a week as a minister of a Baptist church, and the social Gospel approach as a leader of the Urban Seed Café that served addicts and homeless people on the other days. At The Open Gate he discovered that the single flow of compassion that comes from Christ's belly moves into Christ's two arms – the arm of witness and the arm of social care. For the first time he saw how he and others could be holistic Christians.

A fourth example is of Michael Bullock, a South African youth pastor who took a year off to traverse Europe, working for his keep in each pilgrimage place. He wrote:

Lindisfarne was one of the more poignant steps on my journey. Praying one day on St Cuthbert's island, I had the sense of truly being in a coracle – that in truth I had actually pushed away from the shore of my life, and was now upon the vast sea with God. It was a momentous discovery for me because I had been in the mind set of wondering when, if ever, I would have enough courage to push away from the shore. Meantime my very act of pilgrimage had already thrust me out onto waters, and my life will never be the same again …

A father of four teenage sons walked with them across the pilgrim posts. They learned about the four brothers who were among the first twelve students at Lindisfarne's monastic school: Chad, Cedd, Cynibil and Caelin. They asked David Adam to bless them. It was a life-changing visit. Those four brothers each now have vibrant, apostolic ministries. That night the father read the Book of Revelation in Greek in our Celtic Library, lit up by flashes from the lighthouse. Now, his writings light up our world with fresh revelations.

Over the winter of 2012 a young Australian named Joel McKerrow, whose faith had been unraveling for some time, asked if he could stay, along with his wife Heidi. We are normally closed over that time, but we had them stay at The Open Gate and look after themselves. Joel devoured the books in the Celtic library and he began to write his own book, later published as *Woven: A Faith for the Dissatisfied*. In the book he describes the very experience of being on Holy Island as one of the great times of re-weaving of his previously un-ravelled faith. He speaks of how he slowly began to find 'a new weave' within his life, a new home that was, 'found in the walking, not in the arriving … The Woven Self is being called from ahead, not being pushed from behind' (p. 149). Joel describes this time and all that led up to it as when he found 'a tradition that he could belong to' and thus began the reconstruction of his faith and life. He is now one of Australia's most successful touring Performance Poets and has best-selling music/spoken albums. In 2019 he returned to us for a weekend on his UK tour which included a rousing performance in Holy Island's St Mary's Church.

Upon his release from a short prison sentence a young chef in HM Forces vowed to make good his life and walk to a holy island. He thought there was a holy island in Turkey until someone told him there was a Holy Island in Britain. During his three hundred mile walk to Lindisfarne he stopped at a petrol station café, where the store manager gave him a Bible. He began voraciously to read it from the beginning. On his arrival on Holy Island he sat in the church for about four hours waiting for the evening service to begin. After we left the church I invited him to eat something. He slept rough but I gave him a few jobs, and the late Gary, who ran the village store, gave him a few coffees. I told him that the Bible contains two collections of books, and advised him to start with the Gospel accounts of Jesus. I could sense that God was working in the depths of this young man. Before the week was out he informed me that he knew he must walk round the world in silence, as a penance and purification of his violent tongue and actions which had led to his prison sentence, but must first be baptized. He had stayed with the Franciscan brothers at Alnmouth the night before he arrived on the island. I agreed to drive him there, where they would baptize him. Following his baptism he began his vow of silence. I drove him to deserted dunes on a shore. Though not allowed to speak, I felt I must kneel before him and in some way seek the prayer of himself or his angel. Without speaking he urged me to get up. Before he started his silence he said, 'I will see you again'. I do not know the end of this story, but my heart longs to see him again. Meanwhile I pray, 'Dear Jesus, you promised your twelve apostleship they would lead the twelve tribes in heaven: please grant me to wash the feet of ex-prisoners who make reparation by walking round the world in silence.'

The Open Gate was bursting at the seams. Trying to put a quart into a pint pot created stress. We realized the wardens needed to live in a separate house, which would give them space and free up more rooms for guests. David Adam suggested that we purchase an unobtrusive terraced cottage on the edge of the village which was up for sale. A community member purchased this and later, when we could raise a loan, sold it to the Community. After a while living on the top floor of the Open Gate, Carol Few came to live there. She had become the part-time secretary of the dispersed Community while also assisting at The Open Gate. We named the house Shalom.

James and Rosemary Turnbull made a retreat on Holy Island each year. He was a non-stipendiary priest. They had a highly esteemed though unofficial ministry in Glastonbury. Glastonbury is one of Britain's key spiritual centres. Although it claims that Joseph of Arimathea planted a thorn bush there (the monarch is sent a flower from it each Christmas) and that Saint Patrick established a hermitage, it draws devotees of diverse earth spiritualities to the Tor, Chalice Well and the Abbey ruins where the myth that 'King' Arthur was buried there has been promulgated. James spoke prophetically to me: 'Glastonbury needs the deep, pure well of Christian spirituality that Lindisfarne represents: the Community of Aidan and Hilda must make a link with Glastonbury.' This led me to become a Companion of Chalice Well and to visit Glastonbury annually for ten years to lead a retreat, pray and meet with Christian groups or have a book launch. The leader of the goddess movement came to the launch of *Soulfriendship: Celtic Insights into Spiritual Mentoring* (Hodder & Stoughton 1999). She liked the idea of having a soul friend, but not the idea that they had to be Christian. A Glastonbury homeopath wrote to me. He was not a Christian but had read my book *Exploring Celtic Spirituality*. In a dream a Divine Hand had opened his heart and he wept for three days. A local vicar had told him this dream was from the Holy Spirit. Could he come to the retreat I was leading at Chalice Well? He came. There, he read the Bible aloud for the first time in his life.

I climbed Glastonbury Tor and prayed as I sat on the ground with my back against the Tor. Two pagans came up. They had just been for a job interview. They had turned an offer down because they wanted to dedicate their lives to evangelizing for the pagan way of life, where the earth and all people are valued. As we talked I realized they assumed I was a fellow pagan because I was meditating. I decided, with some relish, to continue the conversation as if I was a fellow pagan. They rubbished 'mainline' people for trashing the earth and putting their stuff on to what was natural and tried to commune with the spirits. I told them that I had a problem: I had discovered that the spirits could be selfish or unselfish, just as are humans, so I asked myself how I could find a way of relating only to the good spirits. It was as if I needed to find a conductor for an orchestra in order to establish harmonious music. So I invited Jesus to be the conductor, and he sorted out the true from the false. 'That's a great idea,' one of them said as they walked on to evangelize the world with a new ally. After Rosemary Turnbull was widowed she continued as a faithful CAH Glastonbury member for the rest of her life.

Outside the high season I sometimes travelled and at all times I studied and wrote in spare moments. I owe a debt to my valued friend and colleague Kate Tristram who has a razor sharp academic's brain. Many were the times when I shared with her tentative conclusions of some piece of research, some of which were thereafter re-visited or consigned to the rubbish bin.

To celebrate the new millennium we organized a Celtic Festival on Holy Island with fifty events in diverse venues, including the Village Hall. Charlotte Lobb, whom I had met when I gave talks about Celtic spirituality at the European Union headquarters in Brussels, came for the week. She was no longer in her first flush of youth, and had not married. She went into the 'prayer holes' on the Heugh, and told God that if he wanted her to live as a nun for the rest of her life she was willing. A few days earlier a Northumberland folk singer named Andrew Lobb had rung me. 'I have heard about your festival. I am not a committed Christian but can I play and sing in one of your venues?' I told him the programme was finalized, but he was welcome to busk in the Village Hall between events, when people wandered in to look at art exhibits. After Charlotte told God she was willing to be a nun for life, she wandered into the village hall. The rest, as they say, is history. They had a civil wedding blessing in the Open Gate chapel followed by a glorious celebration.

One day I received a phone call from a highly intelligent German student named Daniel Hug. He had joined the strict Theravada Buddhist Monastery in Northumberland which required eight hours of meditation each day. Daniel decided that he was not a Buddhist. He looked up Holy Island on the internet and discovered that The Community of Aidan and Hilda had a retreat house there.

He informed us he wished to join it! I explained that we were not a residential community and that we had no accommodation for non-guests. He said, 'Then I will sleep at the campsite on the nearby mainland, walk in each day and report for work'. We explained that on some days the tides would prevent this and that, although we had short-term volunteers, we could make no long-term commitment. Daniel borrowed a tent, left his camp site at 3.30 a.m. and reported for duty to our warden, Clare Short, at 7.30 a.m. – not the time she began her working day! We were impressed by his commitment; it reminded us of the importunate widow Jesus commended in his parable. So a cupboard space was found for him to sleep in, and then a caravan. He stayed a year. During this time he set up our first embryo website and asked to be baptized. He insisted that this would be on 26 December and in the sea! Our Vicar, Brother Damian and I jointly baptized him. There was snow on the Cheviot Hills. Damian borrowed some waders from one of our fishermen friends. But Daniel insisted we wade further in so as to be properly immersed. The ocean poured into the waders and several people had to rescue Damian. He was driven the short distance to thaw out in the Vicarage, and I vowed never to perform a Boxing Day sea baptism again. Daniel assured me he was a celibate monk at heart and had no interest in getting married. However, our Secretary, Charlotte invited him to be a godparent at the christening of their baby Yverin. Daniel was mightily impressed by the Lobb family. He told me, 'Perhaps marriage is okay after all.' In due course he met a lovely young woman. They married and had a daughter, Jessica, and joined the Bruderhof Community.

Before that, Josh Campbell, a young Canadian who played professional American football, became a volunteer for a few months. He and Daniel were a study in contrasts. Daniel was tall, thin and ascetic, Josh was rugged and extrovert. Perhaps he sparked in Daniel a need to be competitive, for one wintry day Daniel challenged him to bathe in the sea. Daniel slid silently into the sea, warmed by his contemplative practice; Josh let out a loud scream and stepped straight back onto dry land! A year or two later he and his new wife visited us and I said private prayers for their new marriage.

Our founders had committed us to research early Celtic Christianity and its application for the emerging mission of today. So, my downstairs bed and breakfast room was turned into a Celtic Christian library for use not only by our guests, but by any residents or pilgrims - our aim to stock every serious book in English on Celtic Christianity. Later, Judith Line became the librarian, and has brilliantly catalogued all volumes. Bona fide users (including pilgrims) may search for books on our computer and use the library for study. The Community has provided the premises and a computer, Graham Booth donated some of his books, and I have purchased the three thousand plus new volumes. I have left an endowment for the library's long-term continuance in my will, but hope that a philanthropist will endow us with sufficient to sustain a purpose-built, properly maintained public library.

***

The stairs to my upstairs bedroom were open plan. As a growing number of people came to seek direction or prayer, I found the lack of privacy draining. While I was leading a retreat with Ian Bradley on Iona I was taken to hospital after a bad attack of vertigo. I realized that my open-plan, overcrowded cottage was a danger. I could not be ill there. I also felt that The Open Gate should model our commitment to creation, and it concerned me that we had no home-grown vegetables. I began to look at any house with a garden that came up for sale, in case gifts, loans and the sale proceeds of my house would enable such a purchase.

There were two unexpected but providential developments. Michel Burden, a former vicar of Berwick and his wife Anne owned a terraced house which had a long garden and one of the best views of the harbour and Farne Isles. It was called White House. He had early signs of dementia and they needed to move to a clergy home. One day, out of the blue, he announced that he wanted me to have it. He refused higher offers. At the same time our Community's Caim Council decided they should buy my house and add an extra, private room in order to maintain the library and provide rooms for an Open Gate house-keeper. A Christian friend bridged the gap by arranging an interest-free loan. That Whitehouse garden was the love of my life. I created a vegetable patch although the Open Gate received only a little rhubarb and some gooseberries!

One day Kallistos Ware, the Orthodox Bishop of Diokleia, under the Ecumenical Patriarch, spoke to pilgrims about a theology of creation in the garden of Cambridge House, opposite the Open Gate. I sought his advice. He encouraged Orthodox to make commitments to the Aidan and Hilda Way of Life as part of their spiritual renewal, and affirmed the soul friend as an Orthodox practice, but urged us not to confuse this with Orthodox monastic regulations.

Invitations to speak to dioceses, churches and denominational networks multiplied. I spoke in perhaps a dozen cathedrals and various Catholic monastic centres. I shall always recall how, at the end of a study day hosted by Mirfield, the Anglican monastery in Yorkshire, the prior declared that he had had three conversions in his life and they each began with 'C'. He had been converted to Christ, to computers, and now, that day, to Celtic spirituality! Christopher Chessun, who became Bishop of Woolwich, asked me to help them 'bring the desert into the city'. I held a retreat on this theme in London's Docklands. We used each litter bin we passed as an aid to binning the eight deadly passions.

Following an extended time of serious illness and major surgery, Graham Booth, rector of three parishes on the edge of Nottingham, and his doctor wife Ruth, who had briefly experienced the ministry at the Open Gate felt called to come north. After a while in supporting roles they became wardens and increasingly took responsibility for all the work on Holy Island. Graham was also appointed one of the dispersed Community's Guardians.

Graham and Ruth had a deeply spiritual ministry of encouragement and healing to many, including some who had suffered abuse. They also built a team, encouraging volunteers to share the ministry, and Graham demonstrated practical abilities that were priceless in the complex tasks of building maintenance. While Ruth supported the ministry through her calling and 'tent-making' as a GP she also spent long hours in the Open Gate offering careful listening, friendship, and gentle care to many guests, along with the daily chores of sustaining a ministry of hospitality. Graham also gave himself to the island, chairing the Harbour Committee – one of twenty-three activities in the Peregrini Project that attracted substantial funding. In time they were able to buy their own house on the island, so that now there was a pool of people who loved the island, were available to guests who sought counsel, and gave them a flavour of a praying community.

We now had a centre for spiritual renewal and a Celtic Christianity study facility. We sustained a daily rhythm of prayer: 7.30 a.m., 8.00 a.m. and 5.30 p.m. at St Mary's Church, 12.00 noon and 9.00 p.m. night prayer in our chapel, and we had a core community vowed to live a way of life inspired by island saints. Barely a week went by when someone was not touched by God.

Misunderstandings

That is my side of the story. There are other sides. Brother Damian, who became Vicar of St Mary's used to say 'there are difficulties on Holy Island'. These long pre-dated me. Margaret Thatcher said that to say anything about Northern Ireland was like walking on eggshells. It is like that with Holy Island. There were many issues during my time on Holy Island that brought deep pain, but that chapter awaits to be written. Most of us who live on Holy Island have suffered hardships or wounds. I am not alone.

These were some misunderstandings.

1. Opposition began, unknown to me, before I moved to the island. A Christian worker (and now a friend) asked if he could live in my holiday home at a nominal rent, and I acquiesced. Someone on the island said to me 'These b... born again people are filling up Marygate – we don't want them here'. I froze. I should have said 'I sympathise; tell me how we can help.'

2. The second misunderstanding was that I had come to Holy Island uninvited whereas I had made it clear I would not come to the island unless David Adam welcomed this. But this was not made clear to the islanders for some years.

3. A third misunderstanding was that I wanted to buy up every available property on the island. Apart from the fact that I was penniless, I had always resolved that we should remain a small presence on the island. This misunderstanding followed a severe attack of vertigo and the realization that we needed a house where we could grow vegetables.

John Collins was the island's naturalist. I joined his last midnight nature walk around the island. We held out a sheet, shook a tree, and by torch light identified a multitude of nature's treasures. John fell from his attic and our warden, Ross Peart found him, nearly dead on the ground, called an ambulance and accompanied him to hospital. He saved his life. I visited John in hospital. The one thing he wanted to talk about was nature conservation. He assumed (wrongly as it turned out) that his partner would want to move to the mainland, and he feared lest his nature-friendly garden would be destroyed by commercial property purchasers. Knowing that the Community of Aidan and Hilda was committed to care for creation, he asked if we might purchase the property. I explained that was unlikely, since we had neither the money nor personnel, and wished to maintain only a small presence on the island, but I would see if we could find a way for his wishes for creation to be honoured. In the event, a wonderful project for affordable housing in which residents' applications would have priority – part of the peregrini project – was established. However, the story went round the island that we had tried to take it over!

I did try to learn some lessons. The owner of one gardened property privately told me she would be willing to sell it to me, though she had not yet put it up for public sale. I explained that I needed to sit in the garden and meditate in order to see if it had the right feel. After I did this, the recently bereaved lady next door wrote to the Bishop of Newcastle that I was spying on her house because I wanted to get her out so I could live in it! Our

Open Gate warden, Jean, said, 'Take her some flowers'. I bought the flowers but was terrified that if I crossed the threshold they might call the police. So I sat on the public bench opposite until her grandchildren played outside. I asked if I could bring their gran the bunch of flowers. They all welcomed me in and said they now realized it was a misunderstanding. This taught me the importance of personal contact to overcome misunderstandings. But the house next door was much too expensive.

4. Another misunderstanding was caused by my ecumenical attitude, which had not yet spread to the North East. After two decades engaged in inter-church teamwork at Bowthorpe, with the good will of Norwich Diocese and all the Christian denominations, and after becoming guardian of a dispersed community whose members were from all churches, I naturally contacted the Newcastle Council of Churches Holy Island Working group. Unknown to me, not all church authorities liked working with other churches. So the Working Party welcomed my contact, and asked if it could meet in my house as a non-partisan venue. I realized, however, that the Bowthorpe approach was a world apart from the mentality then embedded in the region. After the Franciscan Brother Damian became vicar he did inspire representatives of the island's three churches and two retreat houses to offer a weekly healing service together. We made a public covenant on Pentecost Sunday. We met weekly to pray for one another and the needs of the island people. This meant a great deal to me and to people who came to the healing services, but it did not outlast Damian's departure.

5. A fifth misunderstanding arose long after I had handed over my responsibilities to Graham. Serious safety concerns were raised about the cellar chapel and the positioning of the large gas tank in the courtyard at the Open Gate. Legislation was changing nationally about the positioning of gas tanks and when our site was inspected Graham was told that the gas company would

no longer supply us while the tank was in the car park. Serious concern was also expressed about gas pipes running through the chapel, and underneath the lounge floor, because of the possibility of leaked gas 'pooling' in that space and the risk of explosion. On top of that, the very worn historic steps into the chapel and the fact that there was only the one entrance and exit also made it increasingly dangerous to continue welcoming ever larger numbers of visitors into that space. There was no alternative space for the chapel and so Graham and others began to work on plans to replace the gas heating system with a more eco-friendly wood-pellet system and to submit a planning application to build a new chapel between the courtyard and the carpark.

A petition and campaign against the chapel became so fierce that it came to the attention of the national press, under the headline, 'An Unholy Row on Holy Island' (22 January 2015 *Daily Telegraph*):

> Holy in name but not in nature' – Holy Island residents say no more churches please. It is seen as the cradle of Christianity in mainland Britain but residents of tiny Holy Island have baulked at plans for a new retreat chapel saying there would be 'too many churches'. It is a problem unimaginable almost anywhere else in Britain as empty churches are converted to trendy wine bars or upmarket apartments.
>
> But for some living on the tellingly named Holy Island in Northumberland the problem, it seems, is not too few churches but too many. Residents of Lindisfarne have tabled objections to plans to allow a small ecumenical retreat centre on the tiny island to build a new chapel. The Community of Aidan and Hilda, which draws inspiration from the lives of the Celtic saints, has submitted a planning application to Northumberland County Council to build a new space for prayer and services at its 'Open Gate' guesthouse on the island. But some of the residents have objected, arguing the island – which has around 200 inhabitants – already has enough churches…

Lindisfarne – also known as Holy Island – is regarded by many as the cradle of Christianity in mainland Britain and has been a place of pilgrimage for more than 1,300 years, as the home of Saints Aidan and Cuthbert. The original monastery founded by Irish monks who had settled at Iona in Scotland had a role in the re-Christianisation of Anglo-Saxon England after the dark ages. The Lindisfarne Gospels, produced between 680 and 720, also helped define a distinctive new Anglo-Saxon style, fusing Celtic and Roman influences.

Many of the objections to the new chapel have been submitted through postcards ... bearing a photo of the Open Gate with the words 'A church too many?' A similar flier has been placed in some windows. X... said some residents believe the island's three places of worship are already enough. She claimed the island is 'Holy in name but not in nature' – with it not having been so since the Reformation in the 16th century – and that for the past few hundred years it has been a fishing community. 'We are a secular community. There are people who go to church. We are not all agnostic or atheist but we are secular.'

The Rev Graham Booth, a guardian of the community, questioned how the island can have too many places of worship, given its famed links with Christianity. But he added: 'We have got no desire to see a spiritual takeover of Holy Island. We are well aware it is an ordinary village community.'

I was in Australia for four months during this campaign and naively thought that this, at least, had nothing to do with me. Little did I know! Someone told me a DVD was produced locally, aiming, it seemed to me, to prove that I wished to take over the island. It made reference to various unconnected pieces of writing of mine: about Sketes (monastic communities) in one place, about villages of God in another, about pilgrim centres such as Holy Island in another. In my opinion these selections ignored my constant theme that such developments should only be where they were welcomed.

My soul friend, and his wife Dorothy, offered valuable insights. Peter advised me to enter a discernment process as to whether I should leave the island. The discernment process encompassed a range of factors. I was getting old. Can one die on the island? The doctor said, 'Of course you can', but five islanders had gone to care homes in Berwick. If I could no longer drive it would be hard to shop for necessities now that supermarkets had replaced island food shops. But the deciding factor was this. Following the furore over building the chapel our trustees wrote to every resident that they understood that behind the campaign was a fear that we might take over the island, so those trustees made a promise not to purchase any more island properties. Now, however, Graham and Ruth had departed and sold their house. The community had no house for replacement wardens. If I moved they could use my house. To a pilgrim who asked, 'What is the point of growing old?' we replied 'To make space for others to grow'. So I reluctantly agreed to leave the island.

I engaged in the Harvard University Implicit Bias online Test. This led me to ponder different views people have of Holy Island. Some people who visit the island on a summer's day forget that if islanders did not fish, farm, clean and cook throughout hard as well as sunny days the island would no longer be a living community. Some visitors come for nature, others for history, and some seek to walk in the steps of Saints Aidan and Cuthbert. If we picture the island as a well, it would be silly to try and insert an artificial base half way up. Jesus said 'I am who I am'. Let the island be what it is, and let us be what we are.

I sympathise with islanders who want to protect the island from incomers who impose their town culture upon it. There are a handful of families whose names are on gravestones and who have often married people from or close to the island. Most of the nasty opposition to us did not come from islanders. One islander told me 'No islander would be against The Open Gate – you have achieved an enormous amount.' Another islander said to me, 'Don't let anyone push you out.' A third islander, who had moved to the mainland, told me that if a person wore a Saint Cuthbert bead around their neck, the island would come to them. I was never able to get a 'bead' (a fossil called a crinoid) with a hole large enough to put a thread through. But late in the day Kayleah found and gave me such a bead. It now hangs on my heart next to our community cross.

I drew up a list to pray for an island resident or establishment each day. Islanders are friends. We draw closer. So, dear islanders, please forgive me for mistakes ....

Two voices hammered at my soul: the voice of Jesus' disciples who urged him not to stay in Jerusalem for fear it would be the death of his cause; and the voice of Christian friends who pointed out that if the persecuted early apostles had not left Jerusalem Christianity would not have spread to the world. Whatever the answer was, in November 2017 I limped out of Holy Island. A sword pierced my heart.

I had to learn to pray like Saint Francis, 'O Divine Master grant that I may not try to be understood but to understand, not try to be loved but to love.' I had to embrace the teaching of the twentieth-century monk Silouan. We must see God's image in every human being. If someone curses me I must remind myself that I brought this upon myself, and be worthy of the curse. This brings inner peace and often melts opposition.

7

Life as an Author

Either write something worth reading or do something worth writing. (Benjamin Franklin)

Academic, lecturer or writer?

I have indicated that I under-performed at both school and college, because of a divided emotional life. I failed one of the London BD papers. Michael Green urged me to re-sit this exam one year into my first curacy, because others who were less bright had passed. I learned, however, that I had to re-sit all the papers, and that the set books had changed. The flexi-university packages of today were then unknown. I decided that I was called to a servant ministry among non-academic working people of Stoke-on-Trent and that I should give all my time and energy to them, so I forfeited my BD.

This question confronted me periodically thereafter. When I began my work with The Community of Aidan and Hilda we pledged to research the Celtic Christian heritage and produce resources. I began to develop some e-study courses. Surely now I should at least get a degree or two with The Open University, for whom I gave some lectures? I consulted Ian Bradley, one of our advisors, whose friendship I have greatly valued over the years, who became professor of cultural and spiritual history at the University of St Andrews. Somewhat to my surprise he strongly urged us not to get enmeshed with a university. He felt that universities lost something when they became detached from monasteries. They lost holistic learning in which head, heart and hands all played a part, which was rooted in the wisdom of God. They were becoming businesses. And in practical terms, we lacked the administrative base to cope with the bureaucracy this would entail.

I think he also felt that the Celtic tradition which we were reviving might offer the world a new paradigm of education. This understanding was re-enforced in me through contacts with Orthodox monastics. Some of them wrote books of authority and scholarship, but they were not part of the university system. They had good brains and carefully-checked sources, but their studies were steeped in prayer and daily reflection, like a dog with a bone, as well as well-stocked libraries. In the USA I saw this motto emblazoned on a school notice board: 'We seek honor not honors.' I thought of the addiction of so many to acquiring academic honors. They could be bought on the internet, and obtained with six-week packages.

I have of course undertaken many courses in varied subjects. I did two years of Clinical Theology at Stoke-on-Trent and courses on spiritual direction. I did short courses on subjects such as time management, team building, Myers-Briggs Personality types, Enneagram and Ignatian spirituality. Our Way of Life commits us to life-long learning. For me that includes not only reading and internet research, but also reflecting back on the day before I sleep, learning lessons from daily life, and keeping a reflective journal.

There was another factor also. I wanted to write books about several different subjects. When I enquired what courses were available on those subjects, I discovered that I would have to devote time to studying things that were not the priorities God had placed on my heart. The courses did not meet the need. I felt that by writing and seeking appraisal from qualified people who shared a similar calling I would better serve God and the cause to which He had called us. I was aware of the danger that I might lack rigour, or fail to ask the right questions or to address criticisms, so I dedicated myself to address these issues. One person to whom I am grateful is my colleague, Canon Kate Tristram, a fine scholar and former tutor at the College of St Hilda and St Bede, Durham, with whom I checked out many matters. The Principal of one university-accredited college told me, when we discussed my becoming an occasional lecturer, that there were two avenues to accreditation as a lecturer. One was university degrees, and the other was published writings. These I had in abundance. Some of my books are designed to be popular. Publishers of popular books dislike many footnotes. Others of my books are more serious and have extensive footnotes.

Lecturer

Invitations came to lead workshops for denominations, to lecture in cathedrals, colleges or church networks in UK, Australia, Canada, Ireland, New Zealand, Scandinavia and USA. The only time in my life, however, when I have received a standing ovation was at the conclusion of a lecture I gave in France at Saint Dol, Brittany, at a colloquium sponsored by the Celtic Orthodox monks there. The ovation was given because I attempted to give the lecture in French! Metropolitan Mael for some reason sent me a French translation of the English text I had mailed him, which he planned to distribute. I joked over the phone that I might as well deliver it in French now and he took me seriously. The Holy Island organist, Beryl, was a good linguist and carefully took me through the pronunciation of the whole text. Whereas Parisiens would have looked down upon my attempts, the Brittany accent was more similar to mine. 'You are not in France, you are in Britain here,' they told me.

I gave the Forrester Lecture at St Andrews University on 'Does the Future Have A Church?' I ended this with words which have become a mantra and which I have often repeated in talks and publications:

- In a twenty-four-hour society, people relate better to seven days a week churches.
- In a multi-choice society people look to churches that offer facilities for a range of temperaments, cultures and ages.
- In the cafe society churches are eating places as well as praying places.
- In a visual, sound-byte age people resort to churches that use different media – poetry as well as pulpits, storytelling as well as sermons.

- In an age of mass travel, when people look for B&Bs and hostels that they can relate to, churches provide accommodation – in their grounds, or on their websites. They once again link up with hostel and guest house movements.
- In a multi-ethnic society people expect to find within the wider church services that are culturally Muslim or Sikh in style.
- In an orphaned society, when mentors, life coaches and growth buddies are in demand in the worlds of business, fitness and AIDS care, people seek out spiritual homes where they can find soul friends and mentors.
- In a packaged, pressured society, suffering from data overload and stressful bureaucracy, people make a bee line for churches where they can chill out, be themselves, have space.
- In a world where equality of regard is written into statutes few people under forty any longer wish to be defined by a protest movement of 450 years ago called the Reformation, but are drawn to churches that are transcending the Protestant or Catholic label.

In Canada I was employed as a 'visiting professor' at Tyndale University College, Toronto. Twice I taught a week's summer school in Celtic Spirituality which was a unit in the students' MA Course. The college kindly recorded these. My friend Oyvind Boyso turned these into MP3's – 'Celtic Christianity: A great course' - which still sells on my website.

I drafted a number of international email courses on subjects such as Celtic Christianity, soul-friendship, new monasticism, desert Christians, Celtic Saints and a Celtic understanding of creation. These were promoted as *'Head through the heart learning* – A link project of the Community of Aidan and Hilda' that relates Celtic Christian spirituality to contemporary life. Each one-year course has been developed by me and Peter Sharpe (formerly Learning Development Officer at Aberystwyth University, Wales).

Most remain in draft form, but Peter has tutored a fair number who have enrolled on the Celtic Spirituality course.

Writer

My father had written one or two unpublished manuscripts and my mother a few short plays. I inherited a love of words, and had a stream of articles published, whether as a student in London University's Sennet newspaper, Tooting and Balham Gazette, or in a hundred monthly parish magazines. At Stoke-on-Trent my Christmas project for juniors, Down to Earth, was included in a resource anthology published by the Church of England (CIO) that was re-printed at least four times. But I had never written a book. I developed a passion to write one. Was this because I had a need to be listened to, or because of a call? I believe it was both.

At Bowthorpe I realised that for a new community to be whole it needed to know its past. I researched how Danes boated down the river and settled in its bow, how Bowthorpe was once a chantry under the auspices of the monastery at Chapel Fields, etc., etc. *Bowthorpe: A Community's Beginnings* (designed by Ian Metcalfe) sold out and has now been incorporated in the larger hardback *Book of Bowthorpe*. If, God forbid, a nuclear holocaust should destroy all my other books, this first book will survive. It was placed, in cellular form, with other documents, in a nuclear-proof container beneath Bowthorpe's Shopping Centre. Grove Books published *How We Grew An Ecumenical Project* in 1984. This is now available as a download on my website. http://www.raysimpson.org/userfiles/file/How_we_grew_a_local_ecumenical_project.pdf.

The first leaders of the Community of Aidan and Hilda identified several foundational aims. These included research into the early evangelisation of Celtic lands, its applications to the church today, and provision of resources. This mandate matched and galvanised what was in my soul. I researched, lived, breathed and wrote about Celtic Christianity. During ten snowed up days in bed with 'flu in my last year at Bowthorpe I drafted a chapter on each of twenty features of Celtic spirituality. I asked two authors for advice.

Michael Mitton suggested I start each chapter with a Bible passage and end with a responsive prayer. Russ Parker urged me to put truths into my own words, not merely to quote others. He arranged for us to meet James Catford, the religious editor of Hodder & Stoughton, at a Cambridge hotel. James asked me to double the number of words and add my personal story. I wanted the book's title to be *Lindisfarne Landmarks*; he, astutely, insisted its title be *Exploring Celtic Spirituality: Historic Roots for Our Future*. However, as we rose to depart Russ pointed to the picture that had hung on the pillar over our heads throughout our discussion. It was of Lindisfarne. 'Is Someone trying to say something?' he asked. James agreed that Part One be entitled *Lindisfarne Landmarks*!

The book evoked a remarkable response. A Cambridge physicist phoned: 'This book is highly significant. It provides the church's agenda for the next thirty years.' He had recently experienced an evangelical conversion. The person who had given him the book was a prophetess trusted by Pope John Paul II. Letters poured in with quotes such as the following:

> *I read it twice in two weeks. Throughout most of my adult life (I'm 34 now) I have been searching for something, something I found in your book. As I read each chapter I felt more and more excited, more and more at home. Here were my own feelings about Christianity put into words... I am convinced that this book will nourish faith and vitalize growth points of the coming generation ...*
>
> *[Your book] has unearthed a cry that has been in my heart for some years now, but I had not been able to recognise what it was until I read it ...*
>
> *After years of loss of faith due to the deaths of her twin daughters and now my brother...my friend has started to come back to life through the light of Celtic spirituality. What brought her back to faith was reading this book.... I feel that I have to write to you to tell you how much I have learned, enjoyed and been influenced by your book, especially Chapter 21, 'One Church' – I was stopped in my tracks when I read this chapter. To me it could stand on its own for the impact it had on my*

*own spiritual path. The line, 'Make your people holy, make your
people one' in the prayer at the end of this chapter made my
heart sing in the hope that it embodied.*

Verbum in Norway and Boedal in Denmark published translations
with a revised foreword by Knut Grunvig. In 2004 Kevin Mayhew
published a revised study edition which has never been out of print.

The embryo community also needed resources. Michael
Mitton said of the liturgies I began to write in the 1990s, 'It is like
a ceaseless stream in you because the well-springs are pure and
deep.' During the succeeding decades that stream of inspiration
has rarely dried up. Yet the maxim that good writing is ten per cent
inspiration and ninety percent perspiration is also my experience.
Hodder published *Celtic Worship Through the Year* in 1997 with a
foreword by Ian Bradley. I love its cover picture of Aidan looking
over Lindisfarne to unevangelised places beyond and I have had this
framed. Many of my readers and new CAH Explorers were hungry
to be fed day by day with Celtic spirituality. So I laboured long and
hard to write *Celtic Daily Light: A Spiritual Journey Through the Year*
which Hodder also published in 1997 and which became a *Church
Times* best seller. We were recruiting Christians who needed to
explore their way of life with a soul friend, but there was a dearth of
soul friends, and few spiritual directors were steeped in the Celtic
tradition. So I wrote *Soulfriendship: Celtic Insights into Spiritual
Mentoring*, which still sells via my website.

While at Bowthorpe, an old friend told me that shortly before
he thought he would die he had a dream that he left an airport
lounge and walked towards the waiting plane carrying one black
suit case inside another and another – like a Russian doll. A steward
told him: 'You cannot be allowed on the plane with all that excess
baggage.' My friend was terrified of dying because he feared that
when layer after layer of his being was stripped away there would
be nothing at the core. We talked about Christ being our core. Some
time later the dream recurred, but this time he walked towards
the plane with nothing but a black leotard! I began to envision the
end of life as an airport departure lounge. We need 'parlours' in
the lounge – parlours of beauty and Bible, friends and forgiveness,

music and memories, poetry and prayer. Soon, this became a book. In 1991 HarperCollins published the first edition of *Before We Say Goodbye: Preparing for a Good Death*. I think it was the last religious book they published before they handed over their religious department to Zondervan publishers. I treasure a letter I received from a family in Galloway who gathered round their departing loved one for her last week. They explained how each day during the last week they lit a candle and read words from the book, held hands and witnessed a glorious departure.

My publishers included HarperCollins and Hodder & Stoughton who had trans-continental distribution networks. They downgraded their religious or non-American departments, however, and were not interested in experimental writing. My writing and the pilgrims who flocked to them were like an ever-flowing stream: what publisher would want an ever-flowing stream? I self-published under the St Aidan Press label *How To Give Yourself a Holy Island Retreat*, but we also needed something to put into the hands of the many pilgrims and visitors to Holy Island for whom it was largely a blank sheet. So I wrote *A Holy Island Prayer Book*. This had four weeks' of readings and prayers for morning, midday and night for each day of the week focused on one place of special interest. David Adam's wife Denise provided line drawings. It was published by Canterbury Press in the UK and Morehouse in North America and has become a bestseller. Although I later contributed a chapter to Canterbury Press's *New Monasticism as Fresh Expressions of Church,* they did not want an ever-flowing stream.

So it was an act of Providence that I met the British publisher Kevin Mayhew by 'divine accident'. One of his composers of Celtic music brought him to Lindisfarne, and knocked on my door. We hit it off, and his company published or re-packaged more than thirty titles until his retirement. I was aware of distribution and other inadequacies, but I valued three things: Kevin's entrepreneurial spirit, his blending of catholic, charismatic and evangelical strands, and his personal touch with authors. When he rang to say that he and his wife Barbara were reading my *Waymarks for the Journey* each day with joy, my heart, too, was filled with joy, as it was when Kevin attended my Life Vows. I went to see him in his and Barbara's lovely Suffolk home in 2018 when he was seriously ill and in a wheelchair; he still had his sparkle.

In 2003 he published the four volume *Celtic Prayer Book*. Volume 1 (*Prayer Rhythms*) comprises prayer services for morning, midday, evening and night for each day of the week and for each church season. Volume 2 (*Saints of the Isles*) contains a prayer, Bible reading and short biography of a Celtic saint for each day of the year. Volume 3 (*Healing the Land*) contains services for natural seasons, enrichment material for sacraments, and services for special occasions such as healing a wounded place or an earth blessing. Volume 4 (*Great Celtic Saints*) contains alternative forms of worship interspersed with stories told by a storyteller.

After these he published a new edition of *Celtic Daily Light*, and what I think is one of the best, but least noted, books I have written, *Church of the Isles: a prophetic strategy for renewal*. I believe the title is to blame: people think it is about the church on a few remote islands. So I succeeded in getting the sub-title extended to 'a prophetic strategy for renewal of the emerging church in Britain and Ireland'. The powers-that-be deleted this in subsequent editions because it was too much of a mouthful. A pity! This book identifies death-marks of Christendom, challenges to the denominations, and features of the emerging church.

The new monastic Celtic tradition that we sought to model includes ceaseless prayer around the clock for everything under the sun. The *Carmina Gadelica* reflects that approach in a nineteenth-century Hebridean islanders' context. We sponsored retreats when people wrote prayers for every aspect of modern life – babies and battered women, computers and cars, holidays and homes, motorbikes and middle age, school and sports, weddings and wounds … I collected the best of these for a book titled *Celtic Blessings: Prayers for Everyday Life*. Loyola Press published both hardback and paperback editions in the USA and Kevin Mayhew a softback edition in UK.

In 2004 Kevin asked me to join a committee of compilers of a major new hymn book for all the churches: *Hymns Old and New - One Church, One Faith, One Lord*. I felt unqualified, but he knew that I was immersed in One Church ways of looking at things, and in the reviving Celtic tradition which also needed to be reflected in the hymn book. We met at the publisher's headquarters at Buxhall, Stowmarket and I stayed in the Swan Hotel, Lavenham.

On one of these visits Kevin arranged for me to record a CD titled *Celtic Journey: An Invitation to Walk Life's Pilgrim Way*. This consisted of five talks each interspersed by a Keith Duke song. It was November, when the blinding sun is low. I drove out of the hotel behind (as I thought) a large truck that had passed. Unfortunately the large truck had a very long, low trailer. I went straight into it. My car had to be taken to a garage and I had to be taken to the recording studio in a shaken condition. I am proud of the fact that, however intently I listen, I cannot discern any tremor or hesitation in the entire CD. It is a beautiful production which has now been turned into a DVD with landscapes of Lindisfarne.

The request to compile a *Celtic Hymn Book* came out of the blue that year. As a musician I am but a hack, but Kevin could think of no one else to ask, and his Celtic CDs were selling fast. Basically, I did an internet search for every Celtic CD worship song, looked at Scottish and Iona hymnbooks, scoured traditional hymnbooks and formed a committee of Celtic musicians, including Andrew Dick, a Church of Scotland minister. The committee tried to define what is Celtic music – an impossible task. We recognized that Celtic hymns have a place for lament, blessing, creation, pilgrimage and celebration of their great saints as well as of praise, and that certain instruments feature strongly in Celtic music such as pipes, harp and bodhran. Musician Keith Duke arranged the hymns for keyboard and guitar, and the Kevin Mayhew music department produced a full music edition for organists and choirs. 'This is not up to standard', I said to David Adam. 'There are some very good things in it', he replied. I was cheeky enough to include twenty-nine hymns or choruses I had composed. Just one of them is I think worthy to be included in classic hymnbooks, but it needs a second verse. It is inspired by the prayer of Aidan's Lindisfarne brothers; the first lines echo a prayer written by a visitor to Holy Island and it goes to the tune of 'Danny Boy':

Here be the peace of those who do your sacred will;
here be the praise of God by night and day;
here be the place where strong ones
serve the weakest,
here be a sight of Christ's most gentle way.
Here be the strength of prophets
righting greed and wrong,
here be the green of land that's tilled with love;
here be the soil of holy lives maturing,
here be a people one with all the saints above.

The Norwegians who visit Lindisfarne love these hymns. They have included some in their song book *Sanger Fra Lindisfarne* published by Verbum.

The hymn book was not published until 2006. The previous year Kevin Mayhew published *A Pilgrim Way: New Celtic Monasticism for Everyday People*. This told the story of the Community of Aidan and Hilda and offered a commentary on its Way of Life. Nine years later he published an updated version with a year's course for groups.

As more people committed to follow a rhythm of daily prayer our worship patterns became more tried and tested. Both Kevin and I felt that a small pocket book, that could be carried around like a breviary, was needed. So that year he also published the pocket book *Everyday Prayer for Busy People*. This has been translated into Danish and Norwegian and is useful for one-off occasions when the Bible readings are included in the text.

Spring Harvest, the large evangelical jamboree, asked me to write a book that gave a biblical and Celtic perspective to questions young people were asking. I collected forty questions asked me by young evangelicals and charismatics, and explored answers. They included theologically dividing questions such as, 'Am I a worm or a royal child?'; 'Should I shun my Muslim work mate as my pastor says, or follow my heart and befriend him?'; 'Can I be a Christian and not believe everything in the Bible?' This proved too radical for the Spring Harvest editorial board, so I had a wasted manuscript on my hands. Kevin Mayhew agreed to publish it, but what should be its title? The clue came when I officiated at a wedding of a friend. The bride's mother attended a community church near Guildford. She sometimes, with others, waved banners and danced during worship, but she had a strong desire to go further and do a somersault! Should she or shouldn't she she asked me. I clarified her motives, and suggested she do it if the worship leaders were happy. She did her somersault! I decided the title of this book should be *Should I Do a Somersault in Church? A Celtic Challenge to Evangelicals and Charismatics.*. This was published in 2006. *A Seeker's Guide to the Christian Church* was published in 2007.

The training and multiplication of soul friends was a constant challenge for us. The community formed a working party which met at The Open Gate. I edited the findings and it was published by Kevin Mayhew in 2008 as *A Guide for Soul Friends: The Art of the Spiritual Companion.*

For some years I was invited by denominational and diocesan networks to resource churches that were looking for tools of transformation. In 2008 I persuaded Kevin, perhaps against his better judgement, to publish *The Transforming Church All-age Programme for Vibrant Renewal.* This consists of a guidebook for leaders and separate log books for children, teenagers and adults in an eleven session course.

I worked on two of my best books that year, and they were published the following year, 2009. *Waymarks for the Journey: Daily Prayer to Change Your World* is a yearbook on our Way of Life. A daily Bible reading, reflection, prayer and next step covers one Waymark for each month. This is a book that can become a bedside companion for years to come. *High Street Monasteries: Fresh Expressions of Committed Christianity* outlines five waves of new monasticism, and translates principles of the ancient Celtic monastic villages into features of 'villages of God' in modern emerging churches. Many people want copies of the virtual village of God diagram from this book and value Simon Reed's appendix on biblical foundations for monastic living.

I developed my own spiritual health test, and transmogrified ascetic practices of Desert Fathers into modern fitness exercises for myself, retreatants and groups I worked with. It was fun working these up into the book *The Joy of Spiritual Fitness: Honing and Toning Your Body, Mind and Soul*, which was published in 2010.

What began in the early 1990's with the churning out of duplicated sheets of Celtic liturgies grew into wide public demand for a solid, comprehensive book of tested liturgies that not only catered for four times a day prayer patterns for each day of the week, but also for each Christian season and – an area that was absent in traditional denominational church worship books – for each of the eight natural seasons in the 'Celtic Year'. I revised my liturgies in the light of feedback from groups who regularly used them, including complaints that seasonal material was not suited to the southern hemisphere, collected or incorporated prayers contributed by other Aidan and Hilda members, and eventually offered this to Kevin Mayhew in 2010. He insisted that the title should be *Lindisfarne Liturgies*. I was not happy, because this book was for the world, not for visitors to one place, however holy, and because of island sensitivities that we were turning the island into our provenance. In the end, reluctantly, I agreed to the title *Liturgies from Lindisfarne*. He also insisted that my name, not the Community of Aidan and Hilda, should be on the front cover. If this was to be usable by churches it needed permission to be reproduced or projected on to screens, so Kevin agreed to publish the book with the text on an attached CD. Although this was a bit pricy, it is actually a bargain for church leaders. We also pressed that this book should be user friendly for community use. We wanted a handy-sized hard-back with ribbon markers. We lost that argument altogether. We've had to settle for an overlarge paperback with no markers.

Good liturgy is an on-going and immense task. As the world becomes more inclusive, our liturgy-users become more diverse and (in the West) the eight highlights of the Celtic Year require liturgies, I made alterations and improvements whenever I stayed in another country and city. And users who were unfamiliar with a church lectionary wanted us to provide a selection of psalms and Bible readings for each prayer pattern. Eventually I produced seven psalms, Old Testament and New Testament readings for every Morning and Evening Prayer. The advancement of the internet age and our new community leadership decided that a CAH Prayer

Book be produced both as an App and in print. A committee was formed. Committees grind on at the pace of the slowest, but publication at last sees the light of day.

Kevin Mayhew is a master of re-packaging. He asked me to make a collection of hundreds of prayers gleaned from all my books. In 2011 he published *Ray Simpson: His Complete Celtic Prayers*. This has proved useful to me, since there is a detailed subject index. He has also produced lots of little prayer books on themes such as *Prayers of Calm, Prayers of Blessing, Prayers for the Journey, Prayers of Love and Peace* and *The Little Prayer Book for Children*. He put a section of *Liturgies from Lindisfarne* into a separate book titled *Lindisfarne Liturgies for Christian Festivals* and has included specific liturgies in books on themes such *as Services for Special Occasions* and *Remember War: Make Peace*.

The early books resourced individuals, later ones resourced churches, and more recent publications seek to resource society. Two books Kevin Mayhew published came entirely from my initiative. While I was writing much on religion and prayer, it was politics that strode across the world stage, dominated public opinion, yet reduced life to competing versions of selfishness. I felt that without the values of true religion our countries were doomed to go downhill. How can you have society without honesty? How can you inculcate honesty if each person is not ultimately accountable to a God of justice who sees all? How can you have a peaceful world without respect? How can you inculcate respect if all people are not designed to reflect the likeness of God who respects us? How can you have society without unselfishness and freedom from envy? How can you inculcate these things without knowing that God is the All-Compassionate One, or that God has revealed himself in human life as Defenceless Love?

I have always been interested in politics. In UK terms I have voted for candidates from all the main parties, sometimes on the basis of their character. The Conservatives believe in capitalism, but capitalism needs to be guided by God if it is not to lead to a society of greed, manipulation and corruption. Socialism needs to be guided by God if it is not to lead to class war, dependency and bureaucracy. Yet the voice of religion is marginalized in our society, or dismissed as in essence the tool of imperialism. That is why I wrote *The Cowshed Revolution: a new society created by downwardly mobile Christians* which was published in 2011. When David Cameron became the Conservative Prime Minister in 2010 he acknowledged that his party had become 'the Nasty Party' because it was run by rich people who did little to tackle huge areas of social need. Instead of calling for compulsory socialism, he called everyone to help build 'The Big Society' in which rich people chose to do voluntary jobs in poor areas. I analysed the six countries with the highest 'well-being' count (mostly Scandinavia and Bhutan) and explored the Catholic concept of the Common Good. This argues that to achieve the Common Good requires governments and businesses to do what only they can do, but also requires every citizen to do what only they can do. Without that, society corrodes. I then looked at the mass appeal of millions becoming Upwardly Mobile, and in the light of Jesus' example, called for a mass movement of comfortable people who choose to become Downwardly Mobile. I gave examples of Christians, movements and social experiments who have done this with good effect.

Over the years I have also contributed items to a variety of Kevin Mayhew books such as *Sermons on Difficult Matters*, *Facing the Issues* and *Faith Matters*. I have written two Lent books (*The Desert and the City* and *Reflective Services for Lent*) and two Advent Books (*Let Dreams Come True* and *Bethlehem's Road*, published in 2017).

CAH encourages members to turn their homes into community houses, but few have so far done so. In 2015 Mayhew published *Houses of Prayer: What they are, where to find them and how to start one*. This reminds readers of a widespread movement of White Houses, inspired by Martin of Tours' White House at Liguges which formed early churches in Britain and Ireland. Another word for church, *kil*, comes from the numerous cells lived in by a hermit, which morphed into the early churches. I was thrilled when my colleagues Graham and Ruth Booth took a stack of books to the Shetland Isles, where they started a House of Prayer on Fetlar.

Now, however, my apostolic passion focused on a gaping need in our Aidan and Hilda world-wide strategy. These two saints were wellsprings, but as our movement spread to other continents followers said, 'Who are they? Why would followers of the Way here want to be associated with these people who came from a past continent of empire?' We had always used the phrase 'Aidan, Hilda and kindred spirits in other lands' in our literature, and it was heartening that, in Australia, for example, indigenous heroes of faith were added in meetings. But I felt people missed some key points. First, Jesus' twelve apostles are five-star saints in churches throughout the world, despite them all being Jews, so the worldwide church should judge 'saints' on their qualities and influence, and on how close they were to the risen Jesus. The second point is that Aidan and Hilda came of different races, language and gender: they combined to become soul friends for the common good. The third point is that they evangelized in an indigenous-friendly way They model a pre-colonial Christianity: this model is needed in a post-colonial age. In summary, Aidan and Hilda are archetypal, and need to be better known. So a passion grew in me to communicate the spirit and story of these two Christ figures for our times.

I wrote endless drafts of a book on Aidan. In the end, I decided it must take the form of my first novel, but I surely lacked the knowledge to write a good novel. I studied books such as Oscar Collier's *How to Write Your First Novel* (Cincinnati, Ohio). Then I providentially met a young man who was one of the script writers for the popular TV series *Holby City*. He urged me to study John Yorke's *Into the Woods: A Five Act Journey Into Story* (Penguin). Yorke asserts that all memorable stories, whether they are classics or TV soaps, have five fundamental ingredients. My friend then introduced me to Joseph Campbell's *Hero's Journey*. This is a Jungian interpretation of the typical journey of a human being through life. It has twelve steps. 1) The hero(es) are introduced; 2) they receive a call to adventure; 3) they are reluctant or at first refuse the call; 4) a mentor encourages them; 5) they cross a threshold and enter a special world; 6) they encounter tests, allies and enemies; 7) they enter the inmost cave, crossing a deeper inner threshold; 8) here they endure the supreme ordeal; 9) they take possession of their reward; 10) they are pursued on the road back to their ordinary life, experiencing some form of spiritual death; 11) they cross the third threshold, and experience a transforming resurrection; 12) they return with the elixir, the secret they have learned, to benefit the ordinary world. I reflected upon a possible scenario for Aidan's early life in Ireland, for his life on Iona, where he has a breakdown after his arrival, and for all we know historically of his life in Northumbria, and shaped his story around these twelve stages in the Hero's journey. I entitled it *Aidan of Lindisfarne: Irish Flame Warms a New World*, in order to appeal to the New World of America, and I found an American publisher, Wipf & Stock, who published this in 2014. This novel ends with 52 pages of historical notes.

BRF published my book *Hilda of Whitby: A Spiritual for Now,* and the Archbishop of York, John Sentamu wrote a foreword. This was well reviewed ('a little gem' wrote the *Church of Ireland Gazette*) and sold well. More to the point, people in Whitby told me it brought a spiritual transformation to their lives. It declares to the world that God can speak to non-believers through dreams.

BRF followed this up in 2016 with a book entitled *St Aidan's Way of Mission: Celtic Insights for a Post-Christian World* by Ray Simpson with Brent Lyons-Lee. As Brent and I sat in a car in Australia's Victoria State we mapped out the chapter headings, which included indigenous mission, life as pilgrimage not possession, soul friends and life-long learning, relationship to the earth, villages of God, women and the spiritual foster mothers, rule and rhythm, social justice and politics. It was largely left to me to write the content. Simon Reed's endorsement on the back cover included these words: 'The Celtic Christians of the first millennium (communicated the faith) with a sensitivity, passion and integrity which led entire kingdoms to Christ. This book, based on deep reflection and down-to-earth engagement, shows us how to follow in their footsteps today.'

Brent Lyons Lee and I co-authored two books for the Australasian public: *The Emerging Church Down Under* and *Celtic Spirituality in the Australian Landscape*.

Anamchara Books, New York, gained permission from Kevin Mayhew to re-cycle some of my existing books and publish some new collections of prayers from 2014. They published *Celtic Spirituality* under the title *Celtic Christianity: Deep Roots for a*

Modern Faith; *Celtic Daily Light* under the title *Daily Light from the Celtic Saints: Ancient Wisdom for Modern Life*, blithely ignoring the confusion this creates in one virtual world. They are publishing a series of prayer collections, including *Prepare the Way: Celtic Prayers for the Season of Light* and (my favourite, which I turn into daily prayer tweets) *Tree of Life: Celtic Prayers to the Universal Christ*.

Over the twenty-five years since the publication of my first full-length book *Exploring Celtic Spirituality*, movements of interest and renewal have mushroomed. So have criticisms. These criticisms range from the serious to the silly. Critics include traditionalists who dislike change, rationalists who dislike imagination, Bible lovers who assume that Celtic means pagan, ethnic purists who think that only those who speak a Celtic language can contribute anything authentic, Augustinians who dismiss today's creation-loving Celts as untrue to the tradition, English church lovers who think that the word 'Anglo-Saxon' should never be mixed with the word 'Celtic' to describe their birthright, historians who can't accept that contemporary religious phenomenology might be as valid a discipline as theirs, new monastics who feel that Facebook Celtic nostalgias cheapen their calling, and 'Celtic' advocates who recant and now claim that Celtic Christianity is neither female – nor creation-friendly. For more than a decade I have collected every serious criticism. I have wrestled with these and tried to sift the wheat from the weeds. After years of work, I crystallised these into twelve major criticisms. I liken this research to mining. I have discarded dross, but deeper down I have found twelve golden keys that can unlock possibilities in a new era. *Celtic Christianity and Climate Crisis – Twelve Keys for the Future of the Church* was published by Sacristy Press in 2020.

A book on *England and Scotland: Sacred Bonds that Transcend Me-First Nationalisms - Saints from the Tay to the Thames* is nearing completion. In the final chapters (see USA, Ireland and Borderlands) I refer to three significant forthcoming writing projects. I also have a few ideas for short books, and some unpublished manuscripts. After the UK Parliament passed the Brexit bill a friend sent a card of Europe's patron saints. 'Don't we need these more than ever?'

she asked. So, just maybe, I will dust up that book on *The Soul of Europe*.

The rest are dreadful, half-completed manuscripts that must never be published. For example, I once had the mad thought to write a half humorous book about Vicars entitled *What's a Vicar, Mum?* It begins as follows

> A little girl on a train saw a seated figure wearing a suit and clerical collar. She asked: 'Excuse me, what are you for?' This book tries to find an answer.
>
> In most countries you have Protestant pastors or Catholic priests. In Scotland you have ministers. But in England they are all vicars these days. Vicars can be men, women, or even bishops. 'Watcha Vicar!' a friendly building worker shouted at the purple-clad Bishop of Norwich. 'I'm not the Vicar, I'm the Bishop' he informed him. 'I know you're the Bishop, Vicar', he replied.
>
> Two centuries ago vicars included great innovators and eccentrics. The *Who's Who* directory was full of them and their enterprising offspring. Nowadays vicars have no time for that sort of thing.
>
> Can vicars be saints? Unlikely – they are far too busy. Which is why only one parish priest has officially been made a saint by the Roman Catholic Church. That man was John Vianney, Curé of Ars, a remote and sparsely populated French parish which gave John time to pray day and night. Another John, who was the busy parish priest of Kronstadt is regarded as a saint by Orthodox Christians. But that's about it...

Blogger, tweeter and podcaster

For most of my life I felt I kept ahead of cultural change. The worldwide web had only just begun when the seven Aidan and Hilda founders first started meeting. I quickly developed e-mailing skills. I owe a debt of gratitude to Kieran Metcalfe of Ascent Creative, who has created and overseen my excellent website, www. raysimpson.org for fifteen years. This has information about all my books, about Holy Island and pilgrimage, a host of free downloads, and weekly blogs. The earliest blog I can trace is 9 September 2007. Since then I have written a blog every week apart from during illness and holidays.

However, progress of social media exploded so quickly, in so many directions, that I fell behind. There were two reasons for this: 1) I am not clever at IT; 2) We were called to remove clutter from our lives, to create spaces for people and contemplation, to renounce the pursuit of celebrity. So abstaining from social media was like abstaining from other addictions. On the other hand I was also committed to obedience; this included obedience to the call to use all means to spread our mission.

At first, like a Pharisee, I condemned Twitter, until I participated in a retreat on the Enneagram run by Dorothy Neilson, author of *Me, God and Prozac: Tools for Tough Times*. I learned that I was an Enneagram Type 4, and that most things in life can be either a curse or a blessing according to how humans use them. At that retreat I resolved that Twitter, etc. could be redeemed. I would open a Twitter account and tweet one prayer every day – and nothing else – ever! Birds tweet with purity of heart. They do not worry how many are listening. Like a bird, who tweets for joy, I would not care if I had a million followers or one, I would tweet my daily prayer first thing upon rising from bed. My German friend Manfred Jahn stayed with me at Whitehouse shortly after I moved in. He offered to set up my Twitter account. He named the account Whitehouse views. My first prayer tweet was: 'May I tweet with the melody of the lark, the wisdom of the owl and the eye of the eagle, in the name of the Holy Dove'. I googled '@whitehouse views'. President Obama and I appeared together. He had over three million followers: I had one! I have sent one prayer tweet on three thousand days ever since.

Nowadays I tweet and email daily, blog and paste this on Facebook weekly, provide a LinkedIn article seasonally and thank God for my weekly assistant Brenda Grace who copes with the rest. The Community has kindly paid for her to work up to 8 hours per week for me – the profits from my website book sales help to re-imburse this. Recently I have recorded YouTube talks and Zoom retreats.

Is my writing an addiction which requires a Twelve Step program to cure it? I have asked myself such questions and have concluded that the answer is no. Writing is a calling, a gift, as well as an art that needs to be worked at every single day. I truly believe that the pen is mightier than the sword. Alexander Solzhenitsyn concluded his 1970 Nobel Laureate speech with these words: 'One word of truth shall outweigh the whole world!'

8

Love of Countries

'I seek to find the soul, the pure essence, of every person, movement and nation – and nurture these.'
I enjoy this sentence of yours very much. (Oyvind)

I went to the International Conference at Caux, Switzerland while I was at theological college. They taught me, 'As I am so is my nation: as my family is so is the world'. I met the American black singer Muriel Smith who sang 'the world walked into my heart'. From that time the world walked into my heart. I loved people from every part of the world. God gave me a love of all countries.

From that time, also the sins of my own country impinged upon my heart.

I have visited most countries in Europe, some in every continent, including seven in Asia (Indonesia, China, Israel, Jordan, Lebanon, Syria and Turkey) but only one in Africa (Egypt), and none in South America. Each country has a unique character. As I travelled to these countries I formed an extra strong bond of love with some. Australia is one, Norway another, and the Republic of Ireland most of all.

Australia

I write about my early visits to Australia in the first chapter of *Emerging Down Under* (atfpress.com). Brent Lyons Lee first invited me to Australia in 2005. I stayed in Geelong three times with him, his wife Belinda and their son Thomas. On my birthday they took me to a café at the end of Geelong pier and asked me to recount my life story. They also invited me to a holiday with Belinda's parents Wendy and Gary by the Geelong sea. On one occasion they took me fishing. I was a failure. I caught just one fish, but it was too small to keep. They told me the Celtic thing to do was to kiss it and return it to the sea!

Before that I made contact with two founding members of The Community of Aidan and Hilda Down Under. The first was heavy metal band leader Brad Bessell, who rang from Adelaide to ask, 'How do I plant a Celtic church in Australia?' He communicated these thoughts to me: 'Under our South Australian desert is the great artesian basin filled with millions of litres of water. The same could be said about the soul of this nation. It seems that church here looks for its nourishment from the seasonal rains that blow in from other countries. It comes and it goes and the land (church) is dry again. I believe that the Celtic Spirituality is not a seasonal rain or trend but something that is deeply buried under the Australian soul like our artesian waters under the desert. It is in the blood of the Scottish, Irish, Welsh, English convicts and immigrants. It just needs to be tapped. I believe that the role of Celtic Spirituality in this nation is to bring healing and reconciliation between the Aboriginal and Non-Aboriginal. In fact, I believe that had Celtic monks come to Australia then the Aboriginal people would have had a spiritual experience similar to that of the ancient Celtic Christians. I also believe the role of the Celtic renewal in this nation is to encourage the Church to embrace a faith that is more gentle and incarnational than the colonial one that we have inherited from our English forebears and less 'salesman-like' than the recent American models that we seem to have embraced.' Brad had dyslexia. I encouraged him. He became a lecturer at Tabor Bible College and a theologian of sorts. On my first visit to him, Pentecostal ministers at Tabor College took me wine tasting in the luscious wine fields of South Australia. It was a memorable experience, but one I have not repeated.

I stayed with Brad and his family three times. Following the first visit he was ordained into the apostolic succession as a member of the Communion of Episcopal and Evangelical Churches which combines evangelical, charismatic, liturgical, and sacramental traditions. On the second visit he was into martial arts and had a job as a bouncer in a night club. His house church consisted of two large families and a boyfriend. Following an hour's praise, and an hour's healing and prayer, Holy Communion and lunch, we went into the park opposite for wrestling.

The second person was Matt Lamont, who was as different from Brad as chalk from cheese. He moved from Perth, where he competed in a strong man competition, to Newcastle, New South Wales.

I met him on Lindisfarne, and then again 'by chance' while I was on Iona. We shared deeply. He told me later that he realized while on those holy islands that he had a choice between strength and wisdom. He chose wisdom. On his return he fell in love with and married a woman whose named means wisdom – Sofia. They had two vivacious girls. He loved nature, and became a contemplative and a Quaker. He re-activated his childhood visits to Boyagin Rock, a place sacred to Aboriginal peoples, where he had divine encounters. He began an inward journey to the heart of his land. This family of four created an annexe in order to be able to offer hospitality. I stayed in the annexe for two weeks. Their garage consists of three sections: 1) a gym with weights; 2) a chapel with Bible and ikons; 3) a hamster home with pop. Holistic!

During my first trip I visited churches, groups, colleges, retreat centres and church leaders in the State of Victoria. These included 'Seed churches' – off-shoots of Urban Seed of which Brent was a leader. I likened Christianity to a two thousand year old tree whose trunk was growing hollow. I invited them to dig into the root system underground, and to draw nutrients from the Scriptures and the Spirit, the saints and the silence, the seasons, the soil and the soul friends. This message seemed to resonate as if its time had come. We met David Tacey, author of books such as *Re-enchantment: A new Australian Spirituality* (HarperCollins Sydney). He suggested to us that Australia is experiencing 'colonisation in reverse': 'The land we thought dull and inert, an empty field upon which we would stamp our own authority, is proving to have a spiritual authority far greater than our own. We are witnessing the rebirth of an ancient experience of the spirit. The spirit is holistic, embodied, mystical, and immanental rather than transcendental. And while the process has only just begun, and will take a great deal more time to be realised, Australia could provide important spiritual leadership to the Western world, because what we are undergoing here is a transformation that all Western nations will eventually have to undergo if civilisation is to recover a creative relationship with the earth … The popular Celtic revival is a positive sign that an earth-based, celebrative spirituality is already growing in parts of the West.'

I felt I could not visit Australia without touching the foot of Uluru, the sacred rock of Anangu people, so I paid for a five-day excursion. I learned some of the Aboriginal dreaming stories, but it seemed to me that the point is not to copy their dreams, but to learn from them how to dream. So I persuaded the driver of the coach which took us from our hotel to the Rock to allow me to stay all day, and only return on the last coach. After an eco-tour with an aboriginal guide round the foot of the Rock, I lingered and dreamed at the Aboriginal Centre. The Bible regards dreaming as part of the movement of God's Spirit among the people: 'Your young will see visions and your old will dream dreams' (Acts 2:17). For me, this is about re-imagining the world with God.

I flew on to New Zealand where I visited Christchurch Cathedral and spoke at a packed meeting at nearby Theology House. These were destroyed in the earthquake a few years later. In Auckland people gathered at the Baptist Church to hear about Aidan, Hilda and a new stirring. The Maori minority is large and better integrated with the Pakeha (White) majority than are most First Nation peoples. The Prayer Book of the Anglican Church, which has a sizeable Maori leadership, has Pakeha services on one page and Maori on the facing page.

My second stay in Australia was in 2011. An inaugural retreat for the Aidan and Hilda Community was held at the Norlane Baptist Church in Geelong (Wathaurong land). This was facilitated by the

well-planned, monastic and child-friendly spaces at Norlane that
Brent had helped to develop. The combination of silent spaces, play,
family life and monasticism was found to be inspiring.

I then flew to Queensland where I met two amazing women.
Heather Johnston and Judy Kennedy. Heather owns substantial
land and some ten properties at Buderim, where her forebears were
part of the settlers' land grab. Heather has taken vows with the
Community. Her habit consists of bare feet, a green 'Healing the
Land' T shirt, Community Cross, and a shawl or skirt, though in
2020 she received the CAH monks' green habit. She regards the
Aboriginal people who once lived there as traditional custodians,
and herself (though owner in current Australian law) also as a
custodian. She seeks to heal the relationship between settlers and
Aboriginals, and to use her properties to reach out to marginalised
people. Heather, with her sister Susie Pitt and brother Dan
entrusted some Bush land as a legally covenanted Nature Reserve in
perpetuity. They each had a third of the remaining land and assets.
Heather formed the Beaulah Community Trust and gave her third
of land to it. The Trust declares: 'We acknowledge the traditional
custodians of the land and their care for it for thousands of years.
We remember that they were forced unjustly from their land. We
bear witness to the pain of that dispossession. Open to the Spirit,
who was always present here, we resolve to appreciate the beauty
of the land, protect its resources, remember its history and honour
its traditional custodians. Beaulah Community Ltd (The Creator
is married to the land).'

Another of the Beaulah properties is being developed to provide
business and employment opportunities for local First People.
All kinds of families within the complex Aboriginal networks
have since returned from time to time to this land. Aboriginal
memorials, artwork and artefacts now grace it, side by side with
a few settlers' memorials. The Archbishop of Perth came for the
opening of a memorial section. A trail runs through this bush land.
A sculpture of Hilda and signposts that include the names of Brad
Bessell (who has done healing of his family tree work there) and
'Ray of Lindisfarne' are near the entrance and a sculpture of Aidan
is being prepared.

Members of the Green House Group are committed to praying together and to responding to local social justice issues. The group accommodates and supports a household of asylum seekers, organises various land care and community building projects, promotes knowledge of the history of early settlement in the wider community and advocates for the acknowledgement and inclusion of Australia's First People on public occasions such as Australia Day and Anzac Day.

Heather rises at 3.00 a.m. and works unbelievably hard. She describes herself as an extreme introvert. She is like an Old Testament prophet. She walks barefoot, shaves her hair and much more. She is intuitive and does not do institutions. Despite this, I would not be surprised if in years to come she is not commemorated along with saints and figureheads.

Judy is another member from Queensland. She and her husband Rod, who has helped to translate the Bible for Torres Strait Islanders, were wonderful hosts to me. Judy leads workshops on writing Celtic-style prayer and poetry at her home. A sample can be downloaded from my website under 'Celtic Prayers Down Under'. She, Rod and Heather regularly shared night prayers on the phone for some years. In the Celtic tradition she encourages children to make up a prayer for everything they do. Her grand-daughter rang her one day and said, 'Granny, I've made up a prayer to say while making the bed'. Judy and Bruce Challenor, whom I got to know in Melbourne, are now the guardians, and dialogue with Aboriginal leaders.

In 2015 I spent four months touring five states. My visa ran out after three months. The solution? Have a holiday in Bali, and get another three months' visa! In this paradise-with-flaws just about everybody sat in a long line along the beach waiting to savour the phenomenon of the sun going down!

Brent and Belinda Lyons Lee and their son Thomas invited me to share their home as the base, which began with a week's holiday by the sea to recover from jet-lag. Brent put huge effort into organizing this five state tour of talks, retreats, hostings and meetings. As a tool for this tour he and I wrote *Celtic Spirituality in an Australian*

Landscape. This was published by St Aidan Press and has been reprinted.

The large evangelical convention *Surrender* was held near Melbourne during my visit. One third of those taking part were Christian Aborigines. Whereas the program for White Australians used clock time, the Aborigines held pow wow in their tents all day: you could drift in and out. I was a speaker at timed events. At one session I introduced the Celtic understanding that biblical Christianity was, despite what hearers had been told, creation-friendly. My talk was scheduled to be followed by a tea break followed by another speaker. However, an Aboriginal from the far-off Northern Territory took the microphone: 'This fella tells you these things. We could have told you these things for hundreds of years.' The organisers gave 'Uncle' the microphone and he talked to us through the tea break.

We thought I could hardly be in Victoria for a month without visiting Raymond Island, in Gippsland, where the Diocese was developing an eco-friendly retreat centre. The Bishop invited clergy from across the Diocese to come and hear about new monasticism. I began my talk imagining Jesus was speaking as follows: 'Welcome to the Abbey of Raymond Island, a place of earth care, wise guardians and spiritual foster mothers. I must pass on soon. I have other places to visit, other flocks to care for. But I cannot leave this island just yet, not until I've licked you into shape; not until you are fit for purpose ...'

I felt home-sick when I left Victoria. For the ensuing months I based with different Aidan and Hilda friends in three other states. In New South Wales I relished the scenery and a house meeting in the glorious Blue Mountains. While I was based with the Lamont family I had an hour with the Catholic bishop of Newcastle, spoke at Newcastle's Anglican cathedral, and at a meeting hosted by Catholic sisters. While there the second CAH Australia national retreat was held at Tahlee, a large Christian camp and retreats site near the north shore of Port Stephens. A local Aboriginal elder welcomed us with a ceremony. All Community of Aidan and Hilda meetings in Australia begin by honouring the traditional custodians of the place where they meet.

Judy and Rod and Heather hosted me in Queensland. Heather had inspired St Mark's Anglican Church at Buderim to hold events that embrace the dispossessed indigenous people. It has used its grounds to create Wany ('Welcome' in Gubbi language) Park. Predator trees planted by white settlers have been removed. I was present when indigenous people planted native trees in their place. The Vicar said, 'Welcome to the church'; the Indigenous people replied, 'Welcome to our land'. I led a weekend on Saint Hilda at the church. Judy arranged for me to do a workshop at Brisbane cathedral, and lead retreats at Brookfields Retreat Centre and elsewhere.

My final leg was in Western Australia, where we had no Aidan and Hilda members. Here my hosts were Beth Roberton and her husband who lived in a woodland home above Perth, the capital city of Western Austalia. I had a day at the University of Western Australia, hosted by Ian Robinson, who organizes pilgrimages through Australia's deserts, and a day at the Anglican Theological College. Beth ran a para-church spirituality network named Dayspring. She organized a week on 'Celtic insights into Soulfriendship' to which church leaders and spiritual seekers came. This resonated so much that she ordered twenty copies of my book *Soulfriendship: Celtic Insights into Spiritual Mentoring* to send to participants afterwards.

This final tour had already been extended to four months when a plea came to extend it by yet one more week and travel hundreds of miles into the desert to Koora Retreat Centre, in Boorabbin National Park. This lies east of the Northern Territory. Koora claims to offer 'monastic cell style accommodation'. Upon our arrival I understood why it was so described; it looked like a scrapyard. By day we had to wear mosquito nets, by night we needed extra blankets to keep out the cold. Nine people had paid good money to book for this retreat on 'A new cradling of Celtic spirituality'. Koora Retreat recognises the cultural and spiritual stewardship of aboriginal Australians who travel through this land from waterhole to waterhole upholding ancient tradition. An aboriginal church stood 160km east at Kalgoorlie. Its pastor was Geoffrey Stokes, who featured in Simon Reeves' TV series about Australia. His wife said to him two days before we began, 'I can sense its time you went walkabout.' So Geoffrey joined us for the duration. On our penultimate day a truck somehow drove us through faint tracks, sending emu and kangaroos flying from our path, until we reached a dry salt lake. Our hosts sat us down on this salt lake. 'You tell your aboriginal stories', they instructed Geoffrey, 'And you tell stories of Celtic spiritual mothers', they instructed me. No notes. No preparation. No escape routes. So this was the new desert/ indigenous spirituality!

Although this tour coincided with a painful 18-month bout of polymyalgic rheumatism, and at one point Brent offered to fly me home, every moment was worthwhile.

Canada

Several visits to Canada have brought to my attention different dimensions to learning. At the first retreat I led on the Quebec border, I was asked to consult with an aboriginal harpist before leading the open-air service of Holy Communion. It was essential that he blessed the land before we began. None of the organizers had realized, however, that he also believed it was essential that he should play his harp before each of my talks, and that I should not begin until he sensed the right moment to stop the music. Intuition, not the clock, helped to shape our learning experience. At a meeting with First Nation Kitari people in Ottawa known as a Smudge I discovered that a feather is handed on to each person in the circle. The person with the feather may tell their story, share their thoughts or stay in silence, without interruption, for as long as they feel is right. When they pass on the feather, the next person has the same opportunity. From such depths of heart-sharings and storytelling wisdom can emerge.

Our Ottawa Explorer, Randal Goodfellow, arranged for me to address the Foresight Group. This consists of Members of Parliament, scientists and business people who advise their constituencies on expected trends over the coming twenty-five years. My visit was the first time they had considered the influence of spirituality. I found this somewhat daunting, especially as the time allocated to me was more than double what I had expected, but I felt a buzz. The reason for this buzz was that the possibility of joined up thinking in politics, science and business and the role of spirituality in this was now on the table. During a visit to the P.A. to one of Canada's political party leaders he told us, 'Politicians will have to take spirituality on board in the future.'

The Sorrento Centre lies amid snow-capped mountains in Canada's British Columbia. It began as a large retreat centre of the Anglican Diocese – now it is evolving into something more. It's late Director, Christopher Lind, told me, 'Christendom is dying; certain places have the seeds of renewal that can make them sustainable in the future.' Sorrento has central accommodation and conference rooms, cabins, campsite, farm, beach, shop, refectory, memorial garden, youth programme, Wi-Fi, sabbatical study facilities and is used by the local community. Chris invited me to lead the annual work week of associates who support the centre. Some of them wonder whether the Centre could evolve into a village of God. We explored early Irish monastic villages of God and holistic Celtic spirituality. I invited them to consider whether a Rule and daily prayer might form part of the centre's evolution. Voyager Dirk Pidcock, a former director, and his wife Karen provided assistance and music for our worship. Dave, the young Jewish farmer, asked us to bless the crops so that they would do well, and we circled the land and their new baby.

A flight from Kelowna and a ferry to Vancouver Island brought me to Victoria, that most civilised capital of British Columbia, where art vendors never press you to buy, musicians grace the bridges, and indigenous history and art are honoured in the streets. Its First United Metropolitan Church hosted a weekend on Celtic Spirituality for the Twenty-First Century. Even the balconies of this large building were quite full. During the Sunday service six screens featured stunning pictures of Lindisfarne – the church was planning a pilgrimage to Ireland, Iona and Lindisfarne. It hosts an all-Canada Greenbelt-type event every Epiphany.

A ferry to mainland Vancouver took me to our friends Gerry and Merry Carol Schonberg (he has a post at Regents College), to their pastor, Tim Dickau, and a lunch and afternoon with about twenty members of their downtown church. Twenty years ago, Grand View Calvary Baptist Church was an aging, commuting congregation. Tim arrived with the vision that they should embrace the neighbourhood and build God's kingdom within it. Members began to buy houses in the neighbourhood. Several large houses are shared, as are organic gardens. Social enterprises have sprouted. The homeless, refugees, sex workers, school kids are cared for. Now they consider whether they should form an intentional community with a Rule. They invited me to tell about the challenges and blessings of our Way of Life and to inter-act with their discussions.

I have only once been invited to be a writer-in-residence in a cathedral. I turned it down. The Bishop and the Dean liked the idea of me spending three or more months writing healing of creation resources, guest preaching, leading courses, etc. The truth is I was appalled by the Anglican church there. It had settled disputes with thriving evangelical congregations in the courts – something Jesus told us not to do. A man called Randy and others took me to students, immigrants and needy groups. The cathedral, however, it seemed to me, was a ghetto in a rich suburb. It excelled in funerals for military VIPs, but cut itself off from the ocean of need in the other half of the city. I explained that CAH was ecumenical, and asked if I could be endorsed by a cross-section of groups. This request was refused, and so I declined.

I travelled several times to Canada where Barb and Bob Hudspith dedicated their farm retreat as an Aidan and Hilda link house, and was twice resident as a lecturer at Tyndale College, Toronto. Tyndale started as a Pentecostal college but grew greatly until now it has students and staff from twenty-six denominations, and is Canada's largest theological college.

One of the students. Andy Groen, invited me to visit the Hamilton House of Prayer, of which he is now director. Inspired by 24/7, this has warm, resourcing relationships with many surrounding churches. Andy kindly drove me on to the breathtaking Niagara Falls before taking me to the airport.

Jesus immersed himself in the river Jordan in order to become one with creation. I immersed myself in the river that carries the life and memory of southern Canada. I met up with Rick Gariepi, who is now working on a website for the Community in Canada. I preached a message to Canada from the outdoors altar of St Mary's Church, March, Ottawa on Trinity Sunday, 2010:

> Greetings from Lindisfarne, the Cradle of Christianity to English-speakers, to you in the land of the Maple leaf, the land of the Trinity…. Moses advised his people to make an altar of earth, so that they would not become pompous and disconnected from creation. Moses would be pleased with you!
>
> The Trinity reveals the humble heart of God … Catch the breathing of The Three … The world faces not only the collapse of falsely-based financial systems, but the collapse of sustainable human life on much of Planet Earth. Suppose we modelled our society on the Fourth R – relationship – the ultimate nature of reality that the Trinity points to? Canada has eschewed models based on greed. It espouses 'Peace, Order and good Government'. Build on that. Grow in the life of the Three: love, honour, trust, co-operation – a way of life you will live and offer to the world.

China

I have visited Hong Kong several times and have crossed into the mainland once. I climbed up to the huge Tian Tan Buddha, completed in 1993, and ate at the nearby Po Lin Monastery. The statue is on Lantau Island and symbolizes the harmonious relationship between humans and nature. I joined one thousand others as they engaged in meditative exercises at 6 a.m. in one of Hong Kong's lovely parks. I visited its university, where visual protests at Beijing's 1989 Tiananmen Square Massacre were prominent. Its population numbers many Christians, and centres such as the YMCA flourish. Yet I sensed that the influences coming in from the mainland threatened to diminish the freedom-loving ethos of this precious Asian stronghold. That led me to invite Beijing residents to join my email course on The Way.

Cyprus

The Diocese of Cyprus and the Gulf invited me to spend six weeks there to nurture its fragile spirituality. The members of each congregation are mainly ex-pats who may employ their own priest to maintain their ex-pat heritage. So the Bishop created a temporary part-time post of Spirituality Advisor in an effort to build up prayer, retreats and spiritual practices. This was an uphill task, but the Spirituality Advisor, my friend Paul Maybury, had 'a divine impulse' to invite me to lead services, quiet days, a retreat for parish members, and one for chaplains at British military bases during Lent.

Although few Sunday churchgoers would attend any week-day event, Paul had an idea. Many had second properties. A different parish would host me for each of the six weeks of Lent. Things might unfold. I might be invited to a meal or coffee for social or spiritual conversation, to a healing or Bible study group or to offer spiritual direction. Elsie and Mike, who lent me their second beach-side home, invited me to meet twelve friends over a fabulous meal at their home. Jan lent me her car. On other days I had coffee or lunch with various clergy and at the YWAM House of Prayer, or I was alone.

Cyprus is the island of saints from the time of St Barnabus, Son of Encouragement. On my first day we visited the final tomb of Saint Lazarus and the monastic cell of St Thekla, the would-be girlfriend of St Paul. Later I stood in the tomb of St Barnabus, Son of Encouragement, in Turkish-ruled northern Cyprus. There I prayed for a host of friends to be encouraged.

At St Barnabas Church, Limassol I preached: 'The Anglican/ Episcopal Communion is not a late add-on to the universal church: its roots are apostolic, holy, orthodox and catholic. The Anglians who invaded Britain (from which we get the name Anglican) inherited a church from the Irish Mission of Aidan, 'apostle of the English'. Aidan's method was to walk among the people. He sought to model God's kingdom on earth. They built little 'villages of God' of daily prayer, learning, hospitality, and work. So is it not an Anglican vision that such a village of God may emerge in a fresh way in Cyprus?'

Edna and Terry hosted me two nights in their village of Ypsonas. We walked two hours round the edge of the Akrotiri base. Linda drove me to the home of herself and her husband Gordon in the village of Pissouri, where they service a church plant. I led the morning prayer service at St Barnabas and next day newcomers arrived via Facebook for an afternoon healing of relationships service. Several people wanted to talk about their vocation.

The apostle Paul travelled from Salamis to meet Cyprus's Governor Sergius Paulus in Paphos. Here I preached in 'St Paul's Pillar Church', so named because the pillar on which Paul was flogged was on this site. The Orthodox allow the Latin Church to be the custodians of this ikon-splendoured church of Ayia Kyriaki, and they let Anglicans hold two weekly services in it. Cyprus is in the Province of Jerusalem and the Middle East. I was loaned a stole from St George's Baghdad.

I had two days of quiet alone in Katafiyio, the two bedroomed 'period cottage' the Diocese rents for people to use for personal retreats. Then a two hours detoured drive to friends with a villa with private guest wing, swimming pool and maid in Nicosia, where I spoke to two stimulating groups.

On Monday we had a tour of Old Nicosia. Jeremy, the Dean of what they say is the world's second smallest Anglican Cathedral, invited me to join eighteen friends and helpers for a delicious evening meal in his home. The travesty of the city cut in two by the barrier between Turkish occupied territory and the rest of the country was brought home to us.

I was allowed through because I had a European Union passport. But the crowds of African students and Turkish Cypriots I spoke to in Northern Cyprus were 'prisoners' in that territory. On Sunday evening I spoke to the mainly African service at St Mark's from the university in Famagusta. Their venue (on loan from the Orthodox Church of St George) is used by varied groups almost continuously throughout Saturday and Sunday in two-hour slots. Pentecostals preceded and Roman Catholics (with a UN chaplain) followed us. I described how our community seeks to recruit and resource 'spiritual athletes' on every continent. St Andrews Kyrenia (Girne) – which on Sunday was host to a Turkish Church, a Russian-speaking service, and the International Church - was also host to we Anglicans. Here I sang, swayed and testified with the congregation of mainly Nigerian students. Ammochostos parish has three churches. Easter Day began for St John's with a beach sunrise service and breakfast, continued with a morning Easter Service during which Orthodox people venerated ikons and I preached, and ended with baptisms in the sea north of the border. The Bishop, I learned, worshipped with the congregation in Baghdad at Easter.

High up among the trees of the Troodos Hills is Machairos Monastery. I had four days' retreat here. My cell had one upright chair, a glass of water, no internet; gates were locked at 6 p.m. the ikons and vegetarian meals were marvelous. There are up to eight hours of chanting each day. I was granted long private conversations with English-speaking monks Joseph and Nephyteos. We explored monastic life, asceticism for people in everyday jobs, spiritual formation under an elder, the church fathers – and they wanted to know about Anglicanism and Celtic saints who nurture lives of holy obedience that speak louder than their words.

We shared our love of Father Sophrony, and of Tolly St Knights Monastery, Essex, where the Cypriot Father Zacharias is an elder. Two early advisors of our Community of Aidan and Hilda, Bishop Simon Barrington-Ward and Franciscan Brother Ramon, were deeply changed in that monastery by the Jesus Prayer, and wrote a little book about its power. Young soldiers walked in. They were permitted to venerate the monastery ikons as part of their duty. So did children on a school trip. 'In Cyprus young people are drawn to the monasteries. Eighty per cent of people at our eight-hour Christmas vigil are young people,' I was told, 'but in Britain you are closing churches down.'

I realised that my original passion for a revival of a 'peoples' monastic life in my own country has too long been submerged under cold water. Their monastery certainly calls for obedience, but each is discipled by their elder (the abbot), who allows their individuality to flower. How can that be? Because obedience is mutual. Through obedience in penance they learn to eschew what impedes their growth in God, but the abbot, through obedience to God in each disciple, encourages each to develop their gifts. A stream of thoughts of what to explore upon my return came to me. But it became clear that the real reason God brought me here was this: to do penance.

Denmark

Although my sister-in-law comes from Alborg, it was Oyvind Borgso who first invited me to this land of 'hygge'. Oyvind is a Norwegian but lives in Denmark. As a teenager he was a tearaway. He went crazy about martial arts. Then he fled to a cave in Syria before its civil war began. There he met Jesus. On his return he developed body-prayer training. He has produced DVDs and a book entitled *Listening to God*. I visited Christiana, which claims to be Europe's largest commune, went north to Jutland to meet a charismatic church and a group of Community of Aidan and Hilda Explorers. I returned to Copenhagen where I spoke at a symposium. I did radio and press interviews and attended Night Prayer by Candlelight in a city-centre church. The Danish publisher Boedal published two of my books.

I had read about and admired the Folk High Schools established by Grundtvig. They provided holistic education for young people who may otherwise have missed out on higher education. Some local communities have taken these over for new community and craft purposes rather than let them close. It was in one of these schools that the Areopagus summer conference took place in July 2017. I was asked to speak about body-mind balance, holistic Christianity and authenticity. During one break in the programme, Betty Taylor flew over from Norwich to witness the first vows of Kitty van Shayk.

Norway

Why do I bond with Norway? A Norwegian suggested to me that the reason England's football team was beaten by Iceland (one England player gets more money than the entire Iceland team) is that the Icelanders did not have outsize egos like the English players, and therefore worked better as a team. Norwegians are the least ego-centric people I know and they love the outdoors. They achieve things because they do not have an inferiority complex. Yet they do not diminish others. The gap between the richest and poorest is not too great – they continue to relate to one another with respect. The book *Spirit Level* lists Norway as in the top six nations that have well-being.

Norway's church is like the last outpost of Christendom. It ceased to be the state church only recently. Around 83 per cent of its youth are confirmed in the church. It has enough income from taxes to pay for organists, youth workers, etc. It dislikes the cult of saints – hence the Community of Aidan and Hilda in Norway tends to call itself Anamcara - yet its church names itself after a mere man: Luther. However, those who have connected with us seek to recover well-springs that were neglected at the Reformation such as pilgrimage, creation, the Desert Fathers and Mothers. They have made links with Coptic monasteries. They have also sought to recover the role of soul friend, though they prefer to use the word *medvandrer* (the mountain guide who accompanies you at your own pace). I have led workshops, retreats, and made friends with all its leaders. Verbum publishers have translated four of my books into Norwegian.

The first members to take vows in Norway wanted to reclaim the pre-Reformation monastic link. So the ancient monastery at Klosters, in Stavanger Diocese, now a museum, was booked. There the local church choir sang and I received the vows of our first voyagers. Nearby is Utstein Klosters. The first time I came here the building was an empty school. Now it is beautifully furnished with guest rooms, chapel and extra facilities. The trustees have visited The Open Gate and we value our links. The first warden, Reidun, became an Explorer.

A candidate in a local government election told me that Norway 'takes' to Celtic spirituality because it never had the feudal system and class war imposed upon it. Like the early Celtic monastic settlements, to which everyone who was part of the extended tribal family belonged, those who live outside cities have a sense of shared belonging. He thinks Villages of God are right for Norway.

In Grimstadt I led soul-friendship weekends. A doctor from an island of over a thousand population said, 'Why can't everyone on our island have a soul friend?' I replied, 'If you could get a thousand people to train in soul friendship on a neighbouring island that would be possible.' Frode invited me to lead a retreat for young people at the Free Lutheran camp and retreat site which was next to a fjord. I told them how Celtic Christians stand in water to pray. They then challenged me to plunge into the freezing fjord at 8.00 a.m. Since then I have been more circumspect! When Frode was youth pastor he invited me to talk to his elders about how churches can grow into villages of God. It is the only time in my life when a church leaders meeting has finished at 1.00 a.m.!

Sven Aasmundveit took over from Tom Martin Bernsten as Anamcara leader. He was Director of the Free Lutheran Studies Centre in Oslo. He invited me to speak at the national conference of the Free Lutherans, and to a camp on an island. Lars Verket came by canoe. He was an outdoor trainer. He climbed the sheer mountainside and placed many lit candles in the crevices for our evening worship. The only other group on the island were the Young Socialists. They were impressed and joined us.

The last bishop whose appointment included a Government vote was Erling Petterson, Bishop of Stavangar. This might have produced tensions with some of his deans who might not have voted for him. He had spoken out with courage against the oil industry's bad effect on the environment and for minorities. In order to build up morale he invited me to lead a retreat for his area deans. He thought that Celtic Christianity might combine evangelical passion with a love of the poor, creation and social justice. They were a marvelous team. Several deans subsequently brought their clergy to retreats on Holy Island.

In 2017 our friends Mecky and Kristin Wohlenberg invited me to join them on a holiday tour. We visited Selje where he had been parish priest. We boated to the island where the Irish or Scottish princess Sunniva had been shipwrecked with other women and had lived a life of prayer. Kristin sang a song that this womb of

Christ's Body in Norway might bring renewed life in our time. We drove up the west coast to Molde, where Solve Hatlen is pastor, and to Alesund, where Jan Lokkeborg was a pastor (they are both in vows) and held meetings in each place. Then far further north to Tromso Cathedral, where the bishop showed us round. People in the southern Bible belt regard the region of Tromso as having mere folk religion. Their patron saint is Olaf, the king who converted people with the threat of the sword. However, she invited us to kneel at the main altar. There I prayed that the cathedral would become the home of a rainbow spirituality that embraced both the Sami people and Celtic spirituality.

Poland

When I worked in East Anglia I was sponsored to make a trip to Poland, where I visited the British and Foreign Bible Society shop in Warsaw. It had been destroyed during World War II, but one wall had been left standing, upon which was written the words 'Heaven and earth shall pass away but my words shall never pass away' (Matthew 24:25). This wall had been preserved as the key feature of the new shop. I then went to Krakow, where I ate something that made me feel like death. A visit to Auschwitz was scheduled. I decided that I must go, even if I died there – this required empathy to a degree I had not countenanced. Auschwitz is etched in my memory – I shall never forget it.

USA

My first USA visit was to Los Angeles. I was invited to preach at its First Congregational Church, which had close links with Hollywood. A previous minister had been Lloyd Douglas, who wrote *The Robe* and *The Big Fisherman*, which became iconic films. At this church they dressed up and processed more than they do at Westminster Abbey! As I stood at the back in my robes, waiting for the procession to begin, an over-dressed woman saw me and shouted at the top of her voice, 'They're all hypocrites here you know'. I gathered that was par for the course in Los Angeles. The church had asked me to preach about 'The Celtic Christmas'. Since nothing is known about this, I discoursed on the fantastic Christmas decorations in the gardens of people like comedian Bob Hope down the road, which included glittering glass angels alongside the reindeer. I suggested the alternative to these was to meet an angel for real. Was my sermon a hit? The only feedback I received was from a down-town lady who said, 'Gee, that was real creepy'!

I saw a bobcat in Yosemite National Park. The Fall in New England was stunningly beautiful. My host Stephen, an Episcopal priest, introduced me to his colleague, whose teenage son had been crushed to death in a farm machine he and his friends had been playing about in. This priest had been to the Toronto Airport church to seek solace, and had lain on the carpet for hours, the Holy Spirit and the spirit of grief upon him in equal measure.

In Evergreen, Colorado, I stayed with the first guardian of our US Community, Jack Stapleton and his wife Dorie-Ann. On another occasion I stayed with friends, and walked into the forest for a day. When a thunderstorm came I just carried on walking under the shelter of the trees. My hosts panicked, however, and called the sheriff. Unknown to me, it was common law that humans escaped the forest during thunder and lightnings! For the first and last time in my life I was shut in a sheriff's vehicle. Fortunately he delivered me to my hosts, not to the jail.

In 2011 the Guardian of our USA NW Pacific Region, Tom Cashman, was engaged in spiritual direction on my last day in Vancouver, and we drove south across the USA border to his home town of Seattle, named after Chief Seattle who declared that 'we did not weave the web of life ... we are all sons and daughters of earth'. Members of the regional group came to the house of Tom and his wife Lyn for a day. Pat Loughery, who manages the USA website, was present. Carol Everson, my host, took me church crawling the following day. We began with her St Columba's Church and ended with packed, twilight Compline in a cathedral, with young people reclining on cushions around the altar. In between we went to The Church of the Apostles, otherwise known as Fremont Abbey.

Fremont is the arty section of Seattle which has declared itself the Arts Centre of the Universe. Some Christians started a Cafe Church in the area. They outgrew it and took over a disused Lutheran-Episcopal Church building opposite. The ground floor is now a six days-a-week arts and music centre with cafe. Upstairs is the worship area. A worship band was followed by an interview with a life prisoner who had gained release. Then there was Open Space. Each person could wander where they wished – to a silent chapel or ikon corner, outside, or to chat in the refreshment lounge. An Episcopal priest was on hand to finish with the prescribed form of Eucharist before they had a meal downstairs.

In 2014 I flew to Albuquerque, New Mexico for the second time. This time it was for the national retreat of the USA Community. It was held at the retreat house of the Catholic Diocese of New Mexico, whose warden, Esther-Marie Nagiel, is CAH guardian of that region. Simon Reed came from London, and our Fresh Expression USA pioneers Cary and Gannon Sims also arrived early. I agreed to cancel my plans in order to do an hour's radio broadcast with Esther-Marie on Catholic Radio. A week later I learned that the Archbishop had banned it from being broadcast because it was too ecumenical. 'You're in good company', I was informed, 'because he's also banned his own Albuquerque priest Richard Rohr from broadcasting.' Despite this waste of a day, I drove 75 miles north to visit Christ-in-the-desert monastery with Simon and the Sims. We drove 13 miles down a dirt track, with a huge drop to our left into the Chama Canyon below. The monks grow their own food and sell their own products, including art work.

I gave talks on The Great Emergence and New Monasticism. We had Forest Church style of worship overlooking the Rio Grande. On our first Saturday we drove one hour north east of Albuquerque to the Jemez Pueblo. Two elders, Sal and Flo Yepa, welcomed us to a meal in their home. Some purchased Flo's quality pottery and we all listened to Sal sing his indigenous hand-drum songs. Although some elders were unhappy about us coming, this thoughtful couple returned another day to our Retreat Centre and sang songs of the Creator before we began our meal. Reciprocal hospitality.

John Paul Martin, who was then USA Guardian, drove me for a full day to Texas, where members of the Community had arranged a programme which helped to defray the costs of my USA visit. Before I left Holy Island I asked my friend Andy Raine to brief me on Texan culture. 'Think big', he said. 'Everything is big'.

I was based at Fort Worth. There are two mega churches in this region, so the 3,000 member Methodist Church which invited me was regarded as a small church. I was given a conducted tour around the premises. Their fifth, huge and most recent organ was proudly introduced. They have five services in various auditoriums each Sunday. I preached at three of the English-language services. A church member who was away let me have her house. I had to be driven along auto-ways to get to this. I enjoyed a meal at a pizza-house within walking distance. The receptionist told me a customer had already paid for it. This unscripted hospitality is a Texas custom.

CAH member Emily Williams organized a Celtic service in her Episcopal church. It began with a young man in a kilt and bagpipes walking up the aisle. He had heard about it and there could be no stopping him. I had an hour's skype conference with Elaine Heath, who was Dean of Duke Divinity. This Methodist leader has started student new monastic house churches.

At the Albuquerque retreat I met Will Toms. He lost his father at the age of five and had an abusive stepfather. As an adult he had a vision of an Indian chief whom he invited to be his father. Will and his Korean wife Millie, who follow Jesus, got a call to ministry among pre-European native peoples, in particular the Hopi people who live in Arizona. They established the YWAM Tribal Winds ministry. Although white Christians have started many churches among native tribes, too often they have failed to look for the Creator's imprints in those tribes and have told Indian converts to ditch their culture and adopt the white person's ways. Will and Millie thought that was wrong. Someone told Will a story that in ancient times a holy man named Brendan sailed from Ireland in a boat made of wood and skins and landed in North America. He followed the One whose name white people translate as Jesus. He may have intended to evangelize, to establish a new paradise like the Garden of Eden in this foreign land. However, when Brendan met the native people he realized that his Jesus was already among them, so, with humility he sailed all the way back to Ireland!

Will thought to himself, 'We need new Brendans, because now we are blind to the Creator's imprints in Indian tribes and we are defacing the Creator's imprints in White society'. Then he learned that CAH includes white Americans who are inspired by Brendan to follow humble ways. They make their vows in a ceremony called The Voyage of the Coracle. Words from Brendan's Voyage are read and a guardian says 'God is calling you to leave behind everything that stops you setting sail in the ocean of God's love'. Tom and Millie invited me over to teach about Celtic spirituality. On my part I pledged to learn about the Creator's imprints in their stories, ceremonies and traditional way of life.

Following our week with the Hopis, we travelled to New Mexico, where we met followers of Jesus involved in native ministries. Then we flew to Oregon and stayed with Randy and Edith Woodley and their son Redbird. Randy, a Keetoowah Cherokee, was director of intercultural studies at George Fox Seminary, Portland. He did extensive PhD research on indigenous beliefs. He concluded that there were enough parallel insights for him to create a construct which he calls The Harmony Way, and which he compares to the biblical understanding of Shalom. He has heard of similar testimonies of a type of harmony way of living from Zulu, Inca, Maasai, Sami, Maori, Inuit, Australian Aboriginal and Hawaiian, as well as from USA Indian people. He concludes that the ancient Semitic shalom construct, or what we can broadly refer to as the Harmony Way, is the Creator's original instruction for the way in which all societies should be ordered, and for how all life on this planet should be lived. Randy invited us to lead a session for his class at George Fox Seminary. He has authored a book *The Harmony Way* (IVP). He trenchantly argues that the American Dream is based on a false premise. It caters to a selfish, consumer-driven mentality that values wealth over justice and peace. He likes to say that every American church is built on stolen land and that if their members really wanted to serve Jesus they would sell their churches and give their money to the indigenous custodians of the land.

That is not likely to become a popular trend! However, in Oregon we were guests of Tom and Nancy Gilbert, members of a Rapture church, who purchased twelve wooden properties around the bend of the river. In a dream God told Tom to ask permission of the local native people. They had died out with western diseases and the US Congress no longer listed any local tribe. Tom researched and tracked down two survivors of the tribe. They had a council and gave him permission to build on their ancestral land. Then God told Tom to donate the amount he had paid for the house to these tribal survivors.

This gesture goes deep. It needs to, because the polarization I experienced in USA was extreme. I vowed never to express any political view while there. Yet even when I asked a factual question I was shouted at. A Republican said, 'Democrats have no moral compass. They kill millions of unborn babies, and subsidise immigrants and shirkers which destroys hard work, enterprise and responsibility.' A Democrat said, 'Republicans have no moral compass. They trample on the environment, the poor and the immigrant. Money is their god.' The values of respect, listening, debate, love and team-building were sorely needed.

This visit prompted three years of reading and writing. The result is that Wipf & Stock will publish *Brendan's Return Voyage – A New American Dream: Indigenous, Post-Colonial and Celtic Theology* in 2021. My prayer is that this, in however small a way, may help to write a new chapter in western democracy.

Ireland

It was not Cork Shopping Centre, which houses our brother's church, that I fell in love with – it was the Irish people, their warm hearts, their sense of humour, the green hills and the sacred landscapes of the Emerald Isle. On my early visits coach drivers would stop at a wayside shrine and pray to Our Lady. Unlike Britain's godless and secular society, faith permeated every aspect of life in Ireland, or so I naively thought. Later I fell in love with the folk memory of first millennium Ireland which became the 'land of saints and scholars'.

Fear also stalked my early visits. Anti-English songs filled the pubs. After The Troubles began in 1969 (when the IRA vowed to militarily defeat the British who ruled Northern Ireland and to kill people in mainland Britain as part of this war) it was foolish to drive in the Republic in a car with a British number plate. I was foolish. I drove through streets which were lined with portraits of UK's Prime Minister Margaret Thatcher being hanged because of her refusal to grant prisoner-of-war status to Bobby Sands and his fellow prisoners in the Maze. The political situation was volatile and if I parked my car to have a snack in a café I would train my eyes upon it in case a bomb was placed under it.

Friends of mine in Moral Re-Armament, who were committed to bring in a 'hate-free, fear-free, greed-free world' worked with a Catholic monastery off the Falls Road which ran through the violence-strewn centre of Belfast. Protestants and Catholics who met there produced a magazine entitled *The Furrow*. I recall a Northern Presbyterian describe that for him repentance meant admitting that he was Irish. I drove through Falls Road and the Protestant Shankill Road when it was littered with burned out cars, not daring to stop. I joined a meeting of peace-makers. During that meeting my car was damaged and its wheels removed.

In order to be able to afford to see my Irish family, and to have free holidays in this land that beckoned me, I took house-for-duty fortnights in Church of Ireland rectories. I met up with a friend of Russ Parker and Michael Mitton, Canon Trevor Sullivan. Beneath his gruff, cigarette-smoking exterior Trevor was a prophet, priest and peace-maker. He listened to God, studied the psycho-dynamics of conflicting groups with networks such as the Tavistock Institute, befriended military, political, community and religious front-liners on all sides of The Troubles. He arranged for Russ Parker to meet leaders of all the parties at a high level secret conference in the Republic, because of Russ's work in Healing Wounded History. Trevor has been a friend and an inspirational model ever since. He invited me to speak at summer schools and meet contacts.

After a period of ghastly atrocities by both sides, both the British and the IRA accepted that a political solution would be better than a military one, Trevor had the thought that groups in three categories, political/military, community and church should meet separately but in parallel, and that they invite the Tavistock Institute to facilitate meetings with the use of their tried and tested methodology. Typically, once they had agreed they could not solve a problem through violence, they identified any next step, any common ground, which they could address. Each said what they felt was the problem, and what needed to be done, without blame, and listened to the other side. Much of these conversations remain secret and Trevor has never divulged information to me.

Once Peace Talks had replaced military warfare he invited me to be the 'Token English' speaker at a Summer School, which included Sinn Fein, the DUP and Irish Government speakers. I said to the ex-IRA speaker, 'I feel so guilty about Britain's record'. He said, 'It's not your fault'.

The first locum I did in a Church of Ireland Rectory was at Glanmire, not far from my family. A Church of Ireland minister in the Republic, Revd Dr Lady Stella Durand became an Aidan and Hilda member: she invited me to do locums in her three churches in County Wicklow. Wicklow has many statues of the heroes in the Great Uprising against British occupation in the 1700s. In one cottage, maintained by Heritage Ireland, where a hero was captured, I prayed with a local for forgiveness and for the healing of wounded memory. Stella arranged for a CAH conference in the Church of Ireland Theological College to which catholic and protestant clergy and laity came.

Trevor often had me over to his parishes of Ballynasloe and Aughrim, where large numbers were slaughtered on both sides of the Williamite and Jacobite wars. Russ Parker and others planted trees of healing in the killing fields. He introduced me to the River Shannon, which is my favourite river in the world. Often I have sat beside it or boated along it to Ireland's Holy Island. Records state that Saint Aidan became the abbot of Scattery Island Hermitage, founded by Saint Senan, in the mouth of the Shannon, and local tradition believes he is the Aidan who later went to Lindisfarne.

So in my novel about Aidan I asked myself where he might have been born and grew up. I place this at an old chief's fort beside the Shannon near Killaloe.

I was invited to lead a workshop at the Pan Celtic Alliance, in Dingle. All workshops were in a Celtic language, and translated into English. They made a single exception for me. I apologized. They said, 'Northumbria is the next best thing to a Celtic land – and we organize pilgrimages to it'. I did a radio broadcast for Radio Eirann. Bishop Trevor Williams, invited me to lead a retreat in Dingle for his large Diocese. Dingle hosted 'Fergie the dolphin'. I had always wanted to swim with dolphins but could not afford Florida rates. At 8.00 a.m. in the morning Fergie brushed against me as I sat at the side of a small boat. That is my closest encounter with a dolphin!

I have, of course, often visited Ireland's great Celtic pilgrimage sites, among them: Armagh, Brandon, Clonfert, Clonmacnoise, Durrow, Glendalough and Skellig Michael. Both Trevor and Russ have friends at Clonmacnoise. I have spoken at two summer schools, conducted a Healing the Land Service, and spent a week of prayer in the Catholic House of Prayer, culminating in a think-tank on a post-Brexit relationship between Britain and Ireland.

'Ray really loves Ireland' a Catholic priest told Graham Booth at a retreat we held in Dublin. That is true. I love its soul, even though it is wrapped in centuries of malformed history laced with Guinness. I felt I had to give something back to its wounded soul and open Britain's eyes to its imperial blindness towards Ireland.

In order for churches to have infrastructures fit for purpose Trevor proposed that the Councils of Churches (which excluded key denominations) be replaced by Churches Together in Britain and Ireland. It is sad that the current leaders of denominations have failed to steer this forward, but it may not be too late.

Trevor was impacted by material in my book *Church of the Isles: A Prophetic Strategy for the Emerging Church in Britain and Ireland*. In this I refer to the Council of the Isles (a nickname for the Council of Britain and Ireland which includes the legislative bodies of the Republic, the four of UK, plus those of Guernsey, Jersey and Isle of Man) which was an off-shoot of the Northern Ireland Peace Process. Currently this lacks teeth, but I argue that, post-Brexit, and if UK breaks up, this could evolve into a federal association with backbone.

For ten years I built up a massive computer file on the psycho-dynamics of the conflicted groups, the history, the stories, the personalities, the healing processes, quotations. Trevor has sent thousands of emails that give links to press, Facebook and academic reports. His torrent of hard-to-decipher one-liners range from 'You twit' to 'Reconciliation: Aidan and Canterbury – sort it out'. He introduced me to the Tavistock Institute which he thinks can help us clarify methodology, systems analysis, problem-solving initiatives and infrastructures; and he inspired me to read academic studies on management of change and conflict, and transforming organisations. Wilfred Bion was a pioneering psycho-analyst whose insights into the psychology of groups informed some of the early participants in the Northern Ireland peace processes and cross-border reconciliation work. He argued that every group has two crucial assumptions. The first is the practical task on the agenda in front of them. The second is the unspoken emotional assumptions that underlie the group. He refers to these as 'basic assumptions'. Basic assumptions consist of: 1) dependency; 2) fight-flight; 3) pairing. He invited group participants to start every meeting by ridding themselves of 'memory, desire or understanding'. He invited them to change 'beta elements' into 'alpha elements'. Beta elements might include raw emotional experiences that are denied or projected on to others. Alpha elements might include conscious understanding, acceptance, working with these in dreams and with therapeutic colleagues. This leads to the ability to tolerate frustration and learn from experience. In the on-going British/Irish reconciliation and renewal processes, 'keeping the space' and awareness of the beta and alpha elements may be keys to the future.

Eventually I crystallized this into a Yearbook entitled *The British and Irish Isles: 366 Unforgettable Citizens*'. The first draft is complete. My hope is that every politician in the eight Administrations, every doctor's surgery and every home in these islands will have a copy and pass the common citizenship tests. My soul friend thinks that this is a quarter of a century ahead of its time, which is why I can find no current politicians or movers and shakers to take it seriously; but we continue searching for foundations, reconciliation charities, networks or newspapers who may sponsor this project.

> *O Ireland, emerald isle in crystal sea*
> *O Ireland, no one bears the mark of Cain like thee*
> *Mountain mist and valley glow*
> *Friendly faces, easy go.*
> *But from the depths of hell below*
> *A broken heart, a deadly blow.*

> *O Ireland, fair maid in Eden's sparkling dawn.*

Paul Kyle
(Used with permission, © Coming King
from the CD *O Ireland*.)

9

Pilgrimage

*Christians must live in perpetual pilgrimage, as
guests of the world. (Columbanus)*

Some of my travels have been in the form of pilgrimages. I
understand why Martin Luther disliked pilgrimages. He thought
it was unhealthy to run hither and thither when the kingdom of
God is within you. Yet the central motif of the Jewish religion
is pilgrimage from a place of slavery to a place of promise, and
the Christian Church was birthed at the Pentecost Pilgrimage in
Jerusalem. The Psalmist says 'blest are those who set their hearts
on pilgrimage' (Psalm 84:5). If we never get off the treadmill of
life we may become prisoners of the treadmill. Generally, I have
felt drawn to pilgrim places where nobodies became somebodies
because they lived for God and loved people. I have frequently been
on pilgrimages in Britain and Ireland. I have made pilgrimage to St
Birgitta's monastery at Vadstena, Sweden, and to the place where
Wenceslas of Bohemia died with words of forgiveness towards his
assassin, and I have mentioned my pilgrimages to Switzerland – but
there have been many more.

Egypt

Although one of my first holidays-in-the-sun was a trip down
the Nile from Aswan to the Valley of the Kings and Luxor, it was
only when the leader of our Community in Norway developed
links with the Coptic church and invited me to meet its Bishop

Thomas that 'holy Egypt' began to grip me. Bishop Thomas is a bundle of energy, innovation and faith. He told us the story of how Muslim Brotherhood members approached in order to burn down his church. He gathered his flock, said he would stay, gave them permission to flee but asked them all to pray before they departed. As they knelt the Lord told him to ask his people to pour liquid soap along the slope the Brotherhood would have to walk down. When they arrived they slipped and slithered on to their backs, and ran off in full retreat! We visited the new Anafura Retreat Centre. Copts were banned from establishing new monasteries. When inspectors came to condemn Anafura, Bishop Thomas took them to the swimming pool. 'Have you ever heard of a monastery with a swimming pool?' he asked them, and they passed on.

On another trip we visited the Cave Church of several thousand. Because Muslims are not permitted to touch pork products, only Christians work in Cairo's vast rubbish dumps. There Father Symeon set up the Cave Church, which holds several thousand on a Sunday. We listened to him give Bible teaching to over five hundred people on a Thursday morning. An Amma has also started a cave church, which the women in our party spent time at. The men stayed at the monastery founded by Saint Macarius in 360AD. It had shrunk in size until Matthew the Poor came to live there. Now it had over a hundred monks and over seven hundred lay workers. At first the fathers did not treat us as real Christians – we were Protestant half-Christians – until they observed that we rose early and shared in the three-hour morning liturgy each day. Then their elders gave us inspiring evening talks and conversation. Their liturgy requires them to read all the psalms. So each of us was given one psalm. We each read a different psalm aloud at the same time! When they 'give the Peace' they breath on one another so we receive the breath of God's Spirit. I realized that Copts are Scriptural and Charismatic – and theirs are quite different to Roman Orders. 'Do you discipline brothers who fail to turn up to the liturgy?' I asked a father. He laughed. 'They came here because they love Jesus. We are brothers. We trust one another. We don't need rules like that' he assured me. Some years later I talked to Norway Pastor Solve Hatlen about these monasteries. 'They can kiss the ring of the elder one minute and make a joke at his expense the next', he said, 'I long for that spirit of intimate family in our churches.'

France

The spiritual care of Ars, the small village in rural France, was given to Jean Vianney (died 1859) because he did not complete his military service and failed his ordination exams. It was thought the church was so remote and had so few members that he could not do much harm there. On his way there the Curé stopped a boy and said, 'If you show me the way to Ars I will show you the way to heaven'. He populated his parish with saints by giving a statue of a saint to every home. He slept little, and prayed much of the night in the church. Seeing the light intrigued the locals. Some were drawn to pray in the church themselves. Once the Curé asked an illiterate peasant what he was doing as he sat in the church looking at Jesus on the Cross. 'He just looks at me, and I just look at him', the peasant replied. That reply has often been used as a template for contemplative prayer. I stayed at a guest house for priests run by nuns, which the Curé had established. I queried whether an Anglican priest qualified to stay there. 'The Church of England is the Catholic Church in England', they assured me. Lourdes was too commercialized. At Lisieux I sat before the Sacrament for several hours silence with two sisters of Saint Thérèse .

Holy Land

I have been to the Holy Land several times, the first as a theological student on a coach trip led by our New Testament lecturer Michael Green. On that occasion I read a copy of the *Times* newspaper while sitting in the Dead Sea!

On subsequent visits I have made sure that pilgrimage embraces Palestinian brothers and sisters and is not 'stolen' by the Israeli Tourist Board. While I was in Jerusalem I took a bus from Damascus Gate to Bethany and walked the original route Jesus took from there to Jerusalem. At the house of Mary and Martha I prayed for our houses, that they would be homes of hospitality where we can wash the feet of Jesus who comes in the guise of others. At the tomb of Lazarus I prayed that souls the world over that are entombed would experience resurrection. When Jerusalem came into view I tried to share Jesus' tears over humanity's blind ways.

I made a point of befriending Christian traders when I was in Bethlehem. One of them pleaded with me: 'Please get the Anglican Church to open a hotel in Bethlehem. All the pilgrim coaches are run by the Israeli tourist office, and apart from one stop at the souvenir shop at Shepherd's Fields they keep out of Bethlehem.' For many years I have supported charities that aid Palestinians. I have yearned that Holy Island, the Cradle of Christ in England, might find a way of twinning with Bethlehem, the Cradle of Christ for the world. I support several Palestinian charities, including the Balfour Project. This reminds us that Britain (through Prime Minister Balfour) promised a homeland to both Jews and Palestinians, but only the promise to the first has as yet been fulfilled.

Malaysia

I visited Malaysia, whose Proclamation of Independence begins 'In the name of God, the Compassionate, the Merciful … the Lord of the universe'. I made my way to Kuala Lumpur's City Forest and its immensely high Visitors' Tower. In its prayer room, to which all are welcome, a Muslim booklet explains that religion, for a Christian, means attending a church service on a Sunday, but for a Muslim it means a way of life. This was an epiphany moment for me. I dedicated all my remaining energies to turning round the monstrous betrayal of Jesus that that statement brought to light.

Medjugorje

Medjugorje is a parish of 2,500 comprising villages in Bosnia and Herzegovina in the war-devasted region near the border in the former Yugoslavia Republic. It became a pilgrimage centre after several young people received regular visions and words from the Virgin Mary. Revd George Tutto suggests that God has chosen this parish to become a lasting 'visible sign' for all to see, a model community for our time, which is hungry for peace and reconciliation. He suggests this for two reasons: they had previously (in 1933) erected a huge cross and dedicated themselves to Christ, and they are at the crucible of deep, longstanding conflicts – both ethnic and ecclesiastical, as recent events confirm. Father Tomislav Vlasic, the then parish priest, reported in 1983: 'In our parish nearly all the families fast on bread and water every Friday. About half of them also fast on Wednesdays. On average in these families, an hour is spent in prayer. The majority of the parishioners come to monthly confession. On Sunday there is a celebration of reconciliation for everyone, not just in the church, but also in the homes where families and neighbours come together to share a meal. A prayer group of some 70 young people meets there three nights a week.'

Dr David du Plessis, the ecumenical Pentecostal leader who was known as, 'Mr Pentecost' wrote: 'In my two days in that village I have never heard an unkind word or criticism of anyone. The whole place is charged with the love of God. You can feel it and you can see it... I saw young people reading the Bible. My conclusion is based on scripture ... The love, unity and fellowship I saw there are only possible in the power of the Holy Spirit.' (Medjugorje Information Centre.)

I joined the first Anglican pilgrimage, which was permitted to pray in the room where the apparitions were received. I wandered through the village and witnessed for myself whole families of three generations praying the rosary together. That is why I went back for a second visit.

Rome

I have been on several pilgrimages to Rome. On that first pilgrimage with Focolare friends we made an act of unity with St Peter (the patron saint of Roman Catholics) at St Peter's in the Vatican, and an act of unity with Saint Paul (the patron saint of Protestants) at St Paul Without-the-Walls. We celebrated a Eucharist in the catacombs.

On the 1400th anniversary of Hilda's baptism at York I was invited to speak at a colloquium at the Anglican Centre in Rome on *Saint Hilda and the Synod of Whitby – a Sign for the Future of the Anglican Communion within a world church that is emerging from a fading Christendom*. This included participants from the Vatican and Rome's Gregorian University. I repeated this anonymous quotation: 'When the English nation was being forged, when the people's gods lost their shine, and the true God began to loom large; when its church was like a chrysalis emerging from its Irish womb but did not yet know how to fly – God placed a shining woman on a throne not made by man at the centre of two worlds no one else could span. Her name was Hilda.'

I pointed out that Hilda was a muse and merciful mother to Christians in both the Irish and Roman traditions, and that no woman in the worldwide church had leadership of men and women in the manner of Hilda for well over a thousand years afterwards. I pointed out that in the Episcopal/Anglican world family African bishops refused to share Communion with American bishops, and that different sides in the recent Catholic world synod on the family would hardly speak to one another. I urged that their common agenda should be to nurture overseers with merciful hearts towards all. I pointed out that Pope John Paul II had a woman muse, and asked if any knew of any woman muse in Rome today. None did. A woman who worked in the Vatican said, 'No one listens to women in the Vatican'. I did not hope to win the argument for the ordination of women in a day. However, when I put forward this foundational theological reason for it: that Christ styled himself the Son of Humanity, and if his Body excluded half of humanity from ordination it denied the Body's fulness, a Catholic theologian said he had never heard that argument before. I did hope to persuade the men to embrace women as merciful mothers, muses, reconcilers and be open to Hilda as a sign of future unity.

Russia

I have made several pilgrimages to Russia. The first was when it was still under Communist rule, and our tourist guides were run by the KGB who had a surveillance person on each floor of the hotel. They took us to Zagorsk, which is now known again as Sergiev Posad, a city northeast of Moscow. The Trinity Cathedral houses the tomb of St Sergius. This saintly monk is known as 'the builder of Russia'. In those days all the churches except one were closed for worship: they were museums. I chose to stay in this church during the lunch break despite the pleadings of the tour leader to go back to our coach. Orthodox women sang intercessions brought from all over Russia. I (somewhat courageously I thought!) wrote in Russian in the visitors' book 'Христос воскрес', Christ is Risen!'.

On another pilgrimage, I gave a talk to members of the Fellowship of St Sergius and St Alban in St Petersburg. I discovered that students at St Petersburg University were learning about St Patrick. I was in email contact with them and one of them translated our CAH Way of Life into Russian, which is still on our website. On another occasion our friend Ken Rundell conducted my sister Sally and I to the monastery island of Vaalem, where hermits form a Skete on the outskirts, and to the monastic city of Pskov. Young people whose parents are atheists now pour into these monasteries, renewed in part by large amounts of money from President Putin. At Pskov, the monastic kremlin had been restored, and included work areas as well as monks' cells. The adjoining main shopping street had a beautiful ikon of Christ with the Samaritan woman prominently displayed on a lamp post. This has something of what I call a village of God.

Singapore

In Singapore I made a pilgrimage to St Hilda's, a large square which includes spaces for traditional and charismatic styles of worship, kindergarten children, accommodation, units let to a mission school, and offices. Colin and Linda Chee welcomed and informed me. Over 27 per cent of Singapore's population of 5.5 million are

Christians – its largest faith community. It could be the Antioch of Asia, sending out missionaries as once Antioch sent out the apostles Paul and Barnabas. Linda was writing a book to celebrate St Hilda's 80th anniversary, was interested in my forthcoming book on Hilda, and wanted to network.

A British church member, Dr Jonathan Robbins, joined us for lunch. Jonathan catapulted from being a boy who never passed an exam to Director of Research and Development in human learning. He was born amid Dorset Celtic Christian roots. He relished our Community's DNA 'to release the song locked in every human heart', inspired by St Hilda and the illiterate cowherd, Caedmon, since his passion is to do the same.

Later I tweeted, 'May Asia's Muslims learn to know Jesus better through Christians who learn from them to pray in the rhythms of the sun'. At present that may be a forlorn hope. For many Singaporeans, like many Chinese Christians, Christianity is a giant productivity drive: there is no time to waste on things such as stillness, contemplation and reflective practices. The time for new monasticism may come a little later there than in the fading Christendom of the West.

Turkey

Seven Community of Aidan and Hilda members – Anglican, Lutheran, Orthodox – and one inter-faith minister came from Norway, UK and USA to spend a week in pilgrimage in Istanbul during Advent 2019, culminating in an hour's audience with his All-Holiness, Ecumenical Patriarch Bartholomew, leader of the world's three hundred million Orthodox Christians.

We also visited Hagia Sophia, the Blue Mosque, churches, including Taizé Prayer at the Dominican Church, and crossed the Bosphorus into Asia. There we prayed near the site of the Council of Chalcedon that the world's religions would discover their eternal home in the Three Loves in God's heart. We were moved to see so many men sitting in prayer in the centre of busy streets. Chalcedon is significant: in order for the Muslim world to understand it the

Christians must repent that a rhythm of daily prayer became divorced from the people through clericalisation.

In a miraculous upper room – the town was heaving and every coffee shop was bursting with people – we prayed and shared together on how we felt the Spirit was calling us to prepare for the meeting with the Patriarch. On the day of the meeting Penny prayed on the floor and it came to her how we should introduce ourselves to the Patriarch: we live in the awareness of the Holy Trinity and that leads us to our love of creation and all people whoever they are; we live aware of the transcendence and immanence of God (words that the Patriarch uses very beautifully in a book he has written) and that the Patriarch is an encouragement to us and we long for love of the Trinity to touch the church in the west.

The Ecumenical Patriarch gave us an hour's heartfelt monastic hospitality. He affirmed our commitment to heal the schisms in Christianity and to heal creation. Of our Three Values (Simplicity, Purity of motive, and Obedience to God in each person) he responded: 'This is authentic Christianity!' He was generous in his monastic welcome, and asked us to meet in his office instead of in the usual throne room.

He is a monk with huge responsibilities, as his desk indicated! He has a focus on saving the planet, peace and poverty. He told us about his world-wide meetings to further ecumenical, ecological and economic partnership based on love, including a recent meeting with the Archbishop of Canterbury to combat trafficking and slavery, and over eight meetings with Pope Francis, and how Francis sends him the coffee he likes!

Each of us was permitted to ask a question. On the question: 'What gives you most joy and what gives you the most pain ?' he talked about the killings of Coptic Christians in Egypt and of others elsewhere, the plight of young people in the secular west; they have to understand that they don't have to give up their faith to be modern; the wars, and the situation in Syria. We were treated with hospitality that we did not dare hope for, and we were told next day that the Patriarch had enjoyed the conversation. We felt we were honoured for the way we live and for our work. We felt a sense of togetherness. We were equals in Christ not children. The Patriarch has written: 'The only viable means of spreading the Gospel is the cultivation of one's own soul to become more spacious to embrace all people'. We saw that in his life and work.

He did not answer David's question: 'When you and Pope Francis. meet do you talk about including women more?' He presented us with books and accepted two of our books, *New Celtic Monasticism for Everyday People*, and *High Street Monasteries*. He asked me to send him any future book I wrote, which I have done.

His personal Secretary, Dimitri, was a wonderfully helpful friend before and after the Sunday Liturgy. He studies Canon Law in Cardiff, and told us the essence of Canon Law is to find the right medicine for different ailments. Frode wants to explore the implications for Norway. Penny gave him my book on The Lindisfarne Gospels which describes the Byzantine influence in these Gospels.

During this hour-long conversation (we had thought we might only have ten minutes) the Patriarch gave us coffee, biscuits, chocolate, crosses, books and pictures, and Penny got a pin! The Patriarch has written: 'The only viable means of spreading the Gospel is the cultivation of one's own soul to become more spacious to embrace all people'. We saw that in his life and work.

Before we left for home we asked the question 'How does this divine dance continue?' We seek to listen to God in order to know the answer. As I prayed in the prayer room at Ataturk airport it came to me that the next such meeting the Community has will not be at the organisational level, it will be in the deep silence of the world's soul – perhaps with a mystic in a desert or in Jerusalem – who knows? Our common vision must be that multitudes of Christians learn to pray daily in public as do Muslims, and that multitudes of Muslims pray with the deepened insight into the nature of Allah which Chalcedon, expressed in today's terms, can bring.

10

The Simpsons

*Trying is the first step towards
failure. (Homer Simpson)*

Once I began to get over my conflicted conscience about leaving Lindisfarne, and 'convalesced' by a Canary Islands' swimming pool for a week, an inner space was created. This enabled things to come to the surface and be attended to. I began to attend to the fact that I was part of the Simpson family.

A family of Saxons who trace their descent from a Saxon lord named Archil somehow managed to reach an accommodation with their Norman overlords and retain much of their land. This is recorded in the Domesday Book of 1086. Their landholdings included the manor of Clint in Yorkshire, and they adopted the name de Clint. At some point in the twelfth century descendants of Simon de Clint adopted the Simpson surname in order to distinguish themselves from the other de Clints. Some branches of this family moved north to Scotland, acquiring lands at Brunton in Fifeshire, and forging close links with the clan Fraser. Simpsons are entitled to wear Fraser tartan, as a titled lady from the Fraser clan assured me at a gathering of Scotland's clans at Holyrood Park. Between 1832-34 *Berwick Advertiser* published its phenomenally successful series *Wilson's Tales of the Borders and Scotland* which tells of Simpsons. They say Simpsons Malt Whisky in Berwick-upon-Tweed produces more whisky than the whole of Scotland! In England, the Simpsons continued to flourish at Mellor Lodge in Derby and Bradley in Durham, but a large branch of the family resettled in the Aylesbury area of Buckinghamshire 100 years before the Conquest, and a thousand years before my parents moved there.

According to *The Origins of the Simpson Family and Their Place in History* published by Lang Syne Publishing, the Simpson motto is *Never Despairing.*

The World Book of Simpsons, a capitalist con if ever there was one, informs me that Simpson means son of Simon, which signifies 'gracious hearing'. The Simpson coat of arms is officially documented in Burke's General Armory. The description of the arms is: 'green, on a gold horizontal band, between three silver crescents in top, and a silver leopard walking, facing the observer, tail between its legs, in base, four black ermine spots. Above the shield and helmet is the crest which is out of a tower, a half lion rampant, holding in both paws a scimitar, all naturally coloured'. Leopards do not change their spots: I hope Simpsons stand for consistency. Lions roar when the majority cower in silence: I hope Simpsons are lion-hearts who speak up for truth.

The Simpson international registry has been developed to determine where Simpson families have migrated. Using a sophisticated network of computer sources in Europe, North America and Australasia over 220 million names and addresses of Simpsons have been located. The most populous area of Simpsons is Lancashire. Some notable Simpsons include Sir James Young Simpson of Edinburgh who discovered chloroform anaesthesia in 1847. His statue is in Princes Street Gardens. His nephew Dr Alexander Simpson inherited his house at 52 Queen Street, and founded the Sunday School union. Today it is a charity called Simpson House which provides a counselling service for adults and children affected by alcohol and drug use. Simpsons have made their mark in Canada. Sir George Simpson was an explorer and administrator of the Hudson's Bay Company. A.B. Simpson, of Prince Edward Island, was founder of the Christian and Missionary Alliance, and is still the inspiration of Pentecostal Presbyterians in the region. One of them has written the foreword to this autobiography.

Some Simpsons have been infamous – think of O.J.. Others have been sports stars. My hero is the mountaineer Joe Simpson, who was thought to be dead after falling into a crevasse in Peru. He managed to crawl back to his base camp and inspired the world through his book *Touching the Void* which was adapted into a film.

But what about my Simpsons? The skeleton in our cupboard is Grandad Simpson.

The 1911 census reveals that Frederick Charles Simpson was then aged 31 and lived at 13 Walbeck Road, Shepherd's Bush. He married Jessie Charlotte Thornback, aged 31, in 1901. They had three children: Jesse Matilda who was at school in 1911, my father Frederick Alexander, and Wilfred. Arnold Schools Admission and Discharges reveal that Frederick Charles Simpson (born 20.5.1874) was admitted to Kenmont Garden School (later re-named Oak Secondary School) in 1882 aged 12 and lived with his mother Jane at 23 Letchford Gardens, Hammersmith, Fulham. From baptism registers we learn that Frederick was baptized on 29.7.1874 at St Marylebone St Mark's Hamilton Terrace. From various registers we learn that Jesse Charlotte Thornback was born 22 February 1874, baptised 2 August 1874 in St John the Baptist Church, Kensington, and that her parents were Alexander and Martha Thornback, 6 Holland Road. Alex's occupation was painter and decorator. She died aged 61 in March 1936 living in Tendring, Essex. Will Probates reveal that Granddad died 1.7.56 at 60 Madeira Road, Holland-On-Sea, Clacton, Essex. The Probate that went to Frederick Alexander Simpson (our Dad) was £4,783 13 shillings and 8 pence. My nephew Sam did online research and visited the Baptist Church in London's Shepherd's Bush which Grandad Simpson helped to build up. My brother thinks the church took in Grandad when he was a boy, and that's where he found his deep biblical faith.

Grandad Simpson moved to Holland-On-Sea as a widower while I was a child. He joined the bowls club and asked a woman named Mrs Bryant to be his housekeeper. She always referred to him as Mr Simpson. One day, on the top of a double-decker bus, he asked her to marry him. 'No, I will not marry you Mr Simpson', she replied, 'but I will continue to be your housekeeper.' On another occasion he was run over by a bus while on his bicycle. An ambulance arrived. He refused to get into it, and instead hobbled in front of it wheeling his bike.

One day I received a birthday card from him. It informed me that he had moved to the seaside in order to die. The clement conditions, however, had prolonged his life. This meant he could no longer afford to send his grandchildren birthday presents – this would be my last! Eventually he did die, and was buried next to his wife Jesse in Clacton Cemetery.

In my twenties I was told by a psychiatrist that some emotional wounds are so deep that we can never gain access to them. It is like living with an amputated leg. But after a dream I thought it might be worth clearing up the Missing Link in our ancestry and to visit the skeleton in the family cupboard. All we were told was that granddad's father was a Very Important Person who on no account must be named. His mother was a West End actress or dancer. One story was that my granddad was sold to a pawn shop.

While my sister was with me one Christmas the TV showed a picture of a forebear of our Queen. 'That's just like a photo of Dad', Sally said. If the VIP Who Must Not Be Named was a senior royal it must have been Prince (later King) Edward VII. So I read a biography of Edward VII. He did indeed have many mistresses, and a house in London where he secretly slept with a different actress night after night. He may have thought it an honour for the lady, but at a time of poverty and deference that raises a question mark. The dates fit the birth date of Granddad Simpson. Sam Simpson thinks the father could not have been Edward VII because the birth certificate names Jane Simpson as a shopper. But what if the actress got a job in a shop, even a pawn shop, while she nurtured her baby?

Ancestry searches reveal that a Miss Jane Simpson performed at the Adelphi Theatre, and that a Jane Simpson lived in a house at 81 Warwick Gardens, Hammersmith with 12 men and 18 women (a boarding house?), including a widow and retired nurse named Sarah Smith. This was quite near Palace Theatre and Queens Theatre (1901 census).

I learned from Philip Magnus' biography of the King that 'the Prince's life, accordingly, continued in its former rut, and it is on record, for example, that Francis Knollys, who shared some of his master's tastes, invited the 26-year-old Lord Rosebery in 1873 to lend his London house (a Google search suggests this was 38

Berkeley Square) as a convenient rendezvous at which the Prince of Wales and the Duke of Edinburgh could meet their euphemistically named 'actress friends'. Rosebery excused himself, but other friends were more accommodating; and cockfighting figured sometimes among the amusements provided'. I learned something else from reading this book – there is no sin that cannot be redeemed.

As I watched the wedding of Prince Harry and Meghan Markle in the castle where Edward lived I shed tears. Especially when I listened to the historic sermon by Michael Curry about love, like fire, being powerful enough to change everything. The future. And even the past. This ban on naming the father seeped into the fibres of the succeeding generations. It was like a curse.

Queen Victoria thought the infant Edward was pure and tender. It was possibly his parents' refusal to let him be schooled with other children his own age which caused him to go into rages, and become a victim of unschooled passions He was neither clever nor chaste, but even Edward had some redeeming features. His first achievement, when international relationships had broken down, was to sustain friendship through yacht meetings with his cousins the German Kaiser and the Russian Tsar, though these efforts failed to avert the first world war which started four years after Edward's death in 1910. His second achievement was to engage with Britain's socially deprived people ('the workers' as the ruling elites patronisingly called them) and put the monarchy on a course that stopped it becoming irrelevant. He was the first European monarch to drive a horseless carriage. I can live with Edward in my DNA, just as we all can live with Adam in our DNA. There is also a new Adam and a King of kings in our DNA. All people are royal children of that King.

Whatever the truth about our forebears, the contemporary Simpsons have made a mark upon the world.

Our mother, Kathleen Simpson (née Todhunter), was educated at Penrhos College in Wales, a boarding school that believed women, as well as men, deserved an all-round holistic education. She was an only child. Her family were staunch Methodists who lived in Winchmore Hill, where her father was, I think, a butcher. She married our father, Frederick Alexander Simpson on June 25

1935 at Winchmore Hill Methodist Church. Mother worked in a bank, but dabbled in writing. Several of her plays were broadcast on BBC Radio 4. I persuaded her to have one of her one-act plays, *The Saint at No.89*, published. It tells of an aged spinster who lived in a squalid apartment whose Christian faith transformed the place. When my parents moved to Woking our father set up his own accountancy practice in London. He, too, dabbled in writing, and met friends at the Wig and Pen Club, where Fleet Street meets the Strand. This was one of London's few architectural gems to survive the Great Fire of London.

Dad's sister Mattie married John Payne. They lived at Jacob's Well, near Guildford. Their only child, Kenneth, studied at Hull University. He became a Roman Catholic and a priest. He is a trustee of the Missionaries of the Poor in Jamaica, which provide basic food, medicines and education for the destitute, indigent and disabled, whom he often visited. He became parish priest at Aylesbury, the Simpsons' ancestral home, and then Administrator of Northampton Cathedral. Following the death of his mother, his father, John, despite being an Anglican, became a much-loved part of the cathedral family. In his old age Ken is priest of St Aidan's, Little Chalfont, in greater London. He gained an affinity with St Aidan and wanted a sculpture of this saint in the church grounds. He gave a photo of the famous Lindisfarne sculpture of St Aidan to an Australian sculptor who re-fashioned this from re-cycled scrap metal. He has written and published many books, including *The Rosary for Today*.

Our Dad's younger brother Wilf married my Auntie Joan. The story is that as students at Kings College, London, all eyes of Wilf and a group of fellow students fell on Joan when they first saw her. They laid a bet as to who would be the first to persuade her to go out with them. Wilf immediately said to Joan, 'I've just won a bet. Will you help me come and spend it? 'Okay', she said, and that was that! They adopted Mark and gave birth to Jane. Jane's children are Judith, Sarah and Matt. Judith is managing editor at Penguin Random House Publishers. Matt has his own building company and loves outdoor sports. Sarah is an educator and school leader with specialism in the field of trauma and mental health.

Jane and her present husband Peter are heart and soul in the village of Goodworth Clatford, near Andover. She helped the village shop and post office to become community-run in accordance with the dying wish of her husband Tony; it now has 60 volunteers. Jane and her husband, Peter, are animators in the local church. Peter is a licensed Reader and Jane, a church warden for seventeen years, is licensed to lead services. During the coronavirus pandemic they sent weekly email letters to the villagers.

Wilf died young, Joan re-married a solicitor named Harold Lake, and they had a daughter Jo. Jo had a great marriage with Barry, a battery service engineer, who sadly died before he reached old age. They had a lovely large family. Her children are Edward, Annabel and twins Sam and Abigail. I am godfather to Annabel, who married a Welsh rugby player named Mark. Jo lives near Jane at Andover.

Nowadays, some people regard it as outdated to use just the paternal surname. I do not wish to under value the Todhunters. My mother's parents had moved to Winchmore Hill, London, from the Lake District. Tod is the Cumbrian name for a fox. John Peel, the infamous hunter of the 'D'ye ken John Peel with his coat so grey' song was grandma Todhunter's ancestor. When Peel's wife, who had already given birth to sixteen bairns, was in labour with twins, and surely needed him by her side, he heard the horn and sped off to join the hunt. What a swine! When my sister Sally and I visited John Peel's grave at Cauldbeck Churchyard years later, it had been vandalized by anti-hunt protesters.

As I mentioned earlier, I have one sister and one brother. Sally gained her BEd at Neville's Cross College, Durham. She rowed for her college and became President of MethSoc, the Methodist Society of Durham University. She spent two years in Jamaica teaching through Voluntary Service Overseas. She persuaded the school where she taught to collect two crocodiles for the pupils to study and nurture. She became a teacher in Bedford, and then worked for the pioneer Asset Re-cycling, which worked closely with the Camphill villages for people with Down's syndrome and other learning difficulties. She befriended one of these, Nigel Hunt, who scribbled accounts of his world. My sister had this published under the title *The World of Nigel Hunt: The Diary of a Mongoloid Youth*. It was the first such account to be published, and Professor L. S. Penrose described it as 'a poignant human document … of considerable scientific interest'. Sally, as you know, joined me at Bowthorpe. She is still heart and soul part of Bowthorpe, but joins me for Christmas week and perhaps a summer holiday. I phone her every Saturday evening.

Her role in Bowthorpe is unheralded but extraordinary. She coordinated pastoral care for many years, and continues to invite people to Sunday and sundry meals. She produces the monthly *Bowthorpe News*, paid for by advertisements, and organises distribution to every household. She took responsibility for twice daily prayer, and has produced a Bowthorpe daily Prayer Book which deserves to be published. She supports the Community Garden and the Chapel Ruin Trust which maintains it as a community resource, and she has given unstinting service to the community workshops. She was the UK representative for Godly Play at various international gatherings. When she retired from official posts there, the workshops presented her with an electric bicycle and a shed in which to lock it. She now has bike-trips to the seaside and nature reserves, and co-ordinates the regional Aidan and Hilda group. When I asked her what she felt God had put her on this earth for she replied in the words of the 1648 Westminster Confession: 'To know God and enjoy him for ever.' She is a saint.

Women in my life

Neither Sally nor I have married. As a young adult in Sussex, although I was not interested in women, certain females were interested in me. At the Burlington Lounge a customer named Ivy became infatuated and I became a sitting duck. Each day she lingered hours over one coffee and followed me home – stalking was not a crime in those days. One day I hastened in the opposite direction. I walked to the far end of the pier. Undeterred, there she was in front of me. 'Stop!' I shouted, 'If you come one step further I will jump into the sea.' She wrote me a letter almost daily.

Eventually I told her: 'I forbid you to write me one more letter.' Two days later I began to receive tape recordings from her in the post! A decade or two later I received a letter from her. She had changed her name and got a divorce. 'Please, please, could we meet just once?' I refused. Was I destroying her destiny or was this a stepping stone towards it?

At Tooting we had a youth fellowship. One member had no boyfriends. She often sidled up to me. Why shouldn't she? But I was not interested. I did, however, begin to feel frissons for several unobtainable women. One was not really an erotic frisson – she was a woman I completely bonded with and I felt we could have stayed in each other's arms for the rest of our lives. She was whisked away by our alarmed host. I took another Tooting friend, a Hindu nurse, on a day out to Bognor. I burned for her as we walked the beach – but she was returning to her family in India the following week! I must be careful what I say about the third woman. In her case I felt both the bonding and the crazy, uncontrollable physical attraction that was like a crank shaft turning inside me. I went as far as asking her parents for permission to marry her. That, too, was doomed. They wanted someone who would join their daughter in the front line of their revolution – not a man of a different class who in their view was in the peripheral enterprise of the church. Did she put her parents before her conviction? God only knows. Generally, however, I am not sexually attracted to women – except women like Brigitte Bardot!

In the 1960s I studied early psychological development, including four years of Dr Frank Lake's Clinical Theology. Dr Lake also experimented in a more controversial area – primal therapy. I enrolled for a week's primal therapy course at Nottingham, I think in the early 1980s. About twelve of us lay on mattresses at his clinic. We had just watched a beautiful slow-motion and much magnified film of sperm flowing from a man's body, entering and fertilizing a woman's egg, growing into an embryo and being born as a baby. As we lay, we listened while Dr Lake told the story of a typical womb journey through its three trimesters. 'Now,' he said, as two kneeling carers held each of our hands, 'I want you to use your intuition; imagine your way into your own unique birth journey, and recount it to your carers.' Each person's re-calling was recorded. The cries of the man on my left were so loud they drowned out much of my recording, but I could not bring myself to throw it away

Across the room a woman went into the primal scream. She had entered the abyss of unbearable pain. I was different. In fact Dr Lake said my response was unique in over two thousand patients. My first trimester was bliss. My soul purred. Here was a space I could return to throughout my life. The second trimester was a totally unexpected explosion into uncontrollable hysteria. My two carers could not hold me: my shrieks of laughter drowned out all other sounds. After that the third trimester is a blank.

Later a group known as *Wholeness through Christ* offered me prayer ministry. A man spoke in a tongue. He thought that my father had 'raped' my mother while I was in the womb, that his sperm had spilled over me and that I took into myself my mother's revulsion. I have no way of checking whether this is fantasy or fact. It certainly fits with the fact that in puberty I repressed sexual desire and the normal way of relating to women became misplaced. But neither should we under-estimate the shock of war being declared as I entered the second womb trimester, and four grandparents being plonked into one house with me on the way.

Dr Frank Lake's primal therapy week at Nottingham did not finish with mere reconstruction of birth experiences. We became aware of continuing reflex actions that resulted from these. Using a Gestalt approach, our inner adult was invited to release our inner child from those conditioned reflexes. I became aware that part of me habitually wanted to run away into a safe womb where I need not deal with difficult decisions. It was immature. However, after one of the final sessions I shouted out: 'Mr Hitler do your worst. I want to be born. It's my earth and my life and I'm going to make the best of it.'

My sister's best friend wrote down her 'guidance' in her daily quiet time. One day she wrote down, 'You will marry Ray Simpson'. She came to live in Norwich. Intellectually, we had quite a lot in common. I had heard of one or two people who had married on the basis of 'God's guidance' and who had only fallen in love after the marriage. When I was informed of this guidance I agreed that, despite my busy schedules, we would meet once a week. According to our puritan conditioning there would be no petting until engagement, and no sex until marriage. Neither she nor I acknowledged my unconscious areas of denial. It appears that she raced ahead in her assumptions. We became engaged and I gave her a ring. I liked her. But my feelings did not flower when we embraced. The date of the wedding was fixed, the Bishop of Norwich agreed to conduct it, and the wedding invitations were sent out. One week before the wedding she cancelled it and returned the ring. I knelt before the ring, weeping, nearly every day for a year. But was I in love with the idea of marriage more than with the person? Vera, our Quaker adherent said, 'You do realize, don't you, that you would have had to choose between your ministry and your marriage?' At the time I did not believe her, but now I think she was right.

Some other women (a large number of whom were older widows!) also fell for me. One of them I liked very much and we worked closely together in the ministry at Bowthorpe. From time to time I felt a physical stirring. She wondered whether we were meant to marry. My three month sabbatical leave was approaching. I said, 'Let's see when I return. If absence makes the heart grow fonder, let's go ahead.' But when I did not see her I did not miss her. I was content to make my sabbath pilgrimages alone. She married someone else.

As an unmarried man in mid-life, older women gathered round and competed for my affections. One woman in a Sheltered Housing centre told me she didn't like Bowthorpe because no one had any brains. I told her 'I don't have brains either.' 'Oh, well,' she replied, 'you speak nicely.' She tried to keep me from leaving her house with varied subterfuges. Once she stood between the door and me and said, 'Have a nut.'

I held a surgery once a week. A three times widowed woman came, and sat in silence. Eventually I said, 'Well, how can I help?' She replied, 'You're in love with me. I'm in love with you. What are we going to do about it?' I could not compete with the late Elvis Presley, however, for the affections of the ladies. One woman came, she informed me, for strictly confidential spiritual direction. 'Elvis has proposed to me,' she confided, 'should I accept?' I won't divulge what advice I gave her, except to say, 'Don't rush into anything'.

Was I gay? There might be a streak – but over the years I concluded that I did not want to be physically joined to anyone, female or male. Was celibacy my vocation? A Religious Sister advised, 'Do whatever most liberates your spirit.' A psychologist told me that in celibacy eros is transformed into agape, a love shared with everyone; he felt that eros and agape in me were touching, but there were still unresolved areas. I have never felt right about making a vow of life-long celibacy. And I have never been able to afford the fees of psychotherapists who are skilled in this area.

Years later, when experts like Dr Az Hakeem created new gender terminology I wrote this:

- My sex (a biological definition): Male
- My gender (a social/psychic self-construct): Masculine.
- My sexuality (defined by who or what I am sexually attracted to): Asexual.

I warmed to youngish men who are virile in body and spirit. Mohammed Ali was once my hero. I warmed to oldish women with outstanding outer and inner beauty, but I did not want sex with them. It seems I am similar to the apostle Paul, who thought it best not to marry if one is not overwhelmed by sexual attraction, and whose passion was poured into apostolic ministry. This can be very satisfying.

During the COVID-19 shut-down I watched the TV series *Robin of Sherwood*. He and Maid Marian were madly in love. On their marriage day she sees him, as she thinks, dead. Heart-broken, she takes vows as a nun. Robin meets her in her convent and explains that she had seen the corpse of his look-alike and begs her now to marry him. She declines, saying, 'I will always carry you in my heart but I am married to God.' The certainty dawned upon me: 'I am married to God.' That is why, I tell myself, on the day I took life vows I purchased a gold wedding ring which I have worn ever since.

The Simpsons in Ireland

I first began to visit Ireland in order to meet up with our brother Tony, his wife Anita and their family in the Republic of Ireland's second city of Cork. They began their Pentecostal church meetings in a mouse and flea-infested room in the city. After a few years of holding meetings in their home, they found larger premises in the town centre which they named The Upper Room Fellowship.

I visited in hospital a woman from their congregation who had been severely injured in a car accident and had been told she would never walk again. She used to speak in tongues and prophesied at an Upper Room meeting that Protestants in Ireland could only be healed when they started to love Jesus' mother. Tony forbade her to come to further meetings. Following the accident she had lain in hospital when a beautiful woman in white came to her and said, 'You *will* walk again'. She understood this woman to be Mary, and she did indeed walk again.

Neither Tony nor Anita believe in modern scientific theory that humans evolved over millions of years from a single organism. Although they do not claim that creation started on the date proposed by Bishop Usher – 23 October 4004 – Anita has recently published a booklet which traces names in the Bible's list of Noah's descendants in a number of accounts from ancient civilisations. Much of these are drawn from Bill Cooper's book *After the Flood: The Early Post-Flood History of Europe* (2015 Creation.com).

Tony and Anita have ministered in Cork all their adult lives. They lost their Upper Room church premises because of a compulsory purchase for a new shopping centre. But they now have perfect fit-for-purpose premises also in the town centre. They put up a notice 'Jesus heals broken hearts'. Next door was Tony and Anita's doctor's surgery. They put up a banner 'Doctors heal everything else'. Irish humour at its best!

From the start they embraced a ministry to Travellers, among whom there is now a move of God. Most couldn't read so Tony and Anita told the Gospel stories through a puppet theatre. Anita has translated a book about the European Gypsy revivals into English. With amazing dedication they have faithfully continued that ministry all their lives. Travellers attended our nephew's wedding, and when Tony and Anita became house-bound during the COVID-19 pandemic they brought them cooked meals on Sundays. Tony has been a speaker at Travellers' Life and Light missions and their Bible School. He has self-published commentaries on books of the Bible including the four Gospels and the Acts of the Apostles, Romans, Philippians and Revelation. In her 80th year Anita received a serious cancer diagnosis. After initial treatments, she eschewed the ongoing medication due to severe side effects, relied on herbal remedies and prayer, and has continued her ministry with gusto!

They have three sons. Sam works for the NGO West Cork Development Partnership which seeks 'progressive, inclusive and engaged communities supporting an improved quality of life for all'. He has been working with the unemployed. He has made several trips to Bethlehem Bible College, and has participated in their conflict-resolution conferences with Israelis and Palestinians. His pastor at Bantry has supported the opening of the St Finbarr's Pilgrim Path and Sam has walked it. He joined a group at Ardmore who have walked the St Declan's Way. They asked me to spend a day with them exploring how they could move from being one-off pilgrims to becoming inner pilgrims every day. Afterwards Sam and I walked past the original foundation of St Declan. Sam married Lesley and they have three children, Fionnula, Dara and Micah. Micah wants to be a footballer, but also a lawyer! Sam takes him to watch a Liverpool game once a year. Dara is an artist and Fionnula wants to lecture in English literature.

Tom married Kemi, who comes from Nigeria's Yoruba tribe. Her grandfather was a chief and her father was a diplomat in the Nigerian High Commission in London. She has recorded some of her poems for Black History Month on Facebook's Africans Connect. Tom works on an oil rig but comes home for weeks at a time. Their four children are vibrant with athletic and artistic energies: Oisin, Donnacha, Rian and Caoimhin, pronounced 'KWEE-vEEN'.

Their youngest son, Peter, went to university in Edinburgh, became a quantity surveyor, but gave it up because he thought no self-respecting person should receive such a high salary. He became a perma-culturist, and married Fiona, who now teaches in the European School in Alicante, Spain. Their three children are Fiachra (named after Ireland's saint of gardening), Cara and Aodhna (pronounced '*AY-O-Nah*') a version of Aidan, meaning Little Flame. Although they mainly live in Spain they regularly come home to Cork. All three are caring fathers.

Fiona's parents were Roman Catholics. When she was a girl she walked past Tony preaching the Gospel in a main street. The only others who did anything public, in my understanding, were so-called charity collectors whose proceeds went to the IRA. Yet the IRA never troubled Tony. They believed that in a united Ireland residents should be free to preach their views on the streets. 'Why is that man doing that?' Fiona asked her father. 'Perhaps he has something to say' he replied. The Legion of Mary, however, did trouble them when they first arrived. They put a letter through their door warning they might be poisoned. Such things are unimaginable now. My brother hired a civic hall to hold a healing crusade led by a well-known Pentecostal healer. It was after the Second Vatican Council. A group of sisters came. 'We've been told we must study the Bible', they informed Tony, 'will you come to our convent and teach us the Bible?'

In August 2006 our three Irish nephews combined to rent a hunting lodge in the Scottish Highlands. Twenty-seven members of 'the Simpson family' came together. We went to the Glenlivet whisky distillery (except for my teetotal brother) where one bottle of whisky cost £700. Since my income in my old age is less than that of someone on the UK's minimum wage, I also bought nothing, but I did enjoy a wee sip. Two years later the Simpsons met up again, this time in Wales's Brecon Beacons.

None of our Simpsons can compare to the fictional Simpsons. We have not been to hell and back like Homer. We have not become the 'listening lady' at the church while the minister had a breakdown as has Marge. We have not been quite as hapless as their three children Bart, Lisa and Maggie. The world's greatest cartoon sit-com was described by critics Alan Sepinwall and Matt Zoller Seitz as '… ambitious, intimate, classical, experimental, hip, corny, and altogether free in its conviction that the imagination should go where it wants.' *The Gospel According to the Simpsons: The Spiritual Life of the World's Most Animated Family* by Mark I. Prinsky prompts this question: How did *The Simpsons*, one of the most popular television shows in history, go from being attacked by many religious leaders for its lack of family values to being called one of the most theologically relevant programs in prime time? Because it gets beneath the surface. I would like to think that the real Simpsons have that in common with Homer, Marge, Bart, Lisa and Maggie: we get beneath the surface.

Sally Simpson, like others in the family, was invited to a Buckingham Palace Garden Party, in her case in recognition of her work in Bowthorpe and for Godly Play. She invited me as her chaperone. The Palace Dress Code informed me I might wear clerical dress. This was the cheapest option. So, in order not to be typecast as merely an Anglican, I wore my brown cassock. A fellow guest, ignoring me, asked her, 'What is he?' A good question. When I lived on Holy Island I described myself as a part-time hermit on a part-time island. When the tide was in I was alone with God: when the tide was out I went out to the world or the world came to me. My twitter account describes me as a Celtic new monastic for tomorrow's world. Perhaps the best description is the title of this autobiography – *Monk in the Market Place*.

My sister thinks I should die grateful, like the biblical Jacob, leaning on a staff, and bless all the Simpson children as he blessed Joseph's offspring.

11

Borderlands

Across the sheen-bright sea
Where seals will bask and geese fly overhead
Aidan's brothers and pilgrims through the ages
Look towards the sun's rising
And see Christ, the True Sun, striding
towards them.
They welcome the endless morning.

Stoke-on-Trent was a depressed area, London a racially diverse area, Bowthorpe a community for all classes and Lindisfarne a place apart. Berwick-Upon-Tweed, my twilight home twelve miles north of Lindisfarne, is none of these – it is a border town. Today, it is England's most northerly borough, but it was once Scotland's wealthiest burgh and greatest port, second only to London. Its commercial and strategic importance put it in the front-line during 300 years of warfare in the Middle Ages. From 1296 to 1482 it changed hands thirteen times between England and Scotland, mostly through force, but twice through royal gift. The local myth is that it is still at war with Russia: when Russia made peace with England Berwick was in Scotland and when Russia made peace with Scotland it was in England! Although Berwick is currently in England it has a Scottish bus service, Berwick Rangers Football Team is in a Scottish League, and opposite my house is the Church of Scotland. When I visited Berwick's Pop-Up Museum's 'Tales of the Borders' I learned that much of this area was once known as

The Debatable Lands, since locals claimed it as their own, and not as part of either Scotland or England.

Now, it is a historic garrison town, surrounded by ramparts, that welcomes tourists. The UK's largest remaining garrison, across the car park opposite me, houses the King's Own Scottish Borderers Regimental Museum. I can step out of my door and walk up the grassy ramparts, there to enjoy sea views of Lindisfarne and Bamburgh, stroll across to the beach, or continue into the historic town centre that overlooks the river Tweed. Most of that river forms the border between Scotland and England, but as it widens into an estuary it is all in England – for the time being at least. This river, that carries so much of the wonder, history and gunge of Scotland flows into and shares it all with England before it becomes purified by the healing salt of the vast ocean that goes to the world. Jesus modelled for us the idea of standing in a river that flows from the Source to the world. As we learn to be as we are, and to flow, we come to a greater reality.

During the 2014 referendum on Scottish independence a poll in a Berwick pub found that 49 per cent wanted to be in an independent Scotland and 51 per cent wanted to stay in England. Or was it the other way round? Some say Berwick has a victim mentality, since it feels neglected by both London and Edinburgh. I urge it to develop a bridge mentality. The Union Chain Bridge across the Tweed a few miles inland is the world's earliest iron suspension bridge. Today we need to build bridges of a different kind.

When I won the school Declamation Trophy I was perhaps not a nationalist, but I was a blind patriot. I was never just an English patriot – I was British. I grew to love Scotland, and Wales as much as England. Some of my best friends vote for Scottish Independence so I maintain with difficulty my life-long practice as Founding Guardian of not expressing partisan views that could obscure the universal imperatives of our Way of Life. However, my feelings about Scottish separatism so consumed me that an alter ego emerged, one James Simpson of Berwick, who wrote to Scottish newspapers and circulated leaflets such as the following:

TEN REASONS TO KEEP SCOTLAND BRITISH

1. Don't destroy Britain – one island bounded by a silver sea has existed for thousands of years.
2. We share one language, one geography, one currency, one faith, and one history.
3. If Scotland retains the pound it will become the puppet of the Bank of England without representation in the UK Parliament.
4. If Scotland adopts the Euro it will require tariff controls at over 300 roads and all airports and ferries – a costly bureaucratic nightmare.
5. UK is in the world's top 10 economies. 70% of our common wealth comes from the City of London. Without this Scotland would not even be in the top 100 economies: poverty, disease and crime would multiply.
6. Scottish monarchs also reign over England, Wales and Northern Island – why cut out parts of your own head? Independence would require yet another referendum on whether to retain the monarchy and whether to join the Commonwealth.
7. Racism is a sin. British non-Scots were wounded by racist slurs during the 2014 Independence Referendum. The wounds are still healing. Ban racism. Forgive past mistreatments. Heal wounds.
8. Most black and brown immigrants regard themselves as Black or Brown British citizens. Don't destroy this precious Diversity in Unity. British Lives Matter!
9. The last referendum question was slanted. It should have been 'Should Scotland leave the UK?' If the half million Scotland-born residents in England would be granted Scottish citizenship why deny them a vote? Since the British identity of the majority in UK will be destroyed, why deny them even an advisory vote?
10. If, instead of thinking of itself as the smaller, overlooked third of Britain, Scotland thought of herself as the head

of a body, this could foster a healthy and confident self-image to everyone's mutual benefit.

James Simpson seriously contemplates emigrating if Britain breaks up. Ray Simpson would not countenance this or circulate such material. He is, however, happy to point out that if Scotland became independent Berwick would be the only county town of a shire (Berwickshire) that is in a foreign country. More importantly, he calls every people to be prejudice-free.

In the autumn of my life globalism has impregnated the world. Internationalism – freedom to trade, travel, befriend, study the world over (if you have the money and can get travel visas) has on the whole been a blessing. It has also become a curse, because 99 per cent of the wealth is now controlled by 1 per cent of the population. This 1 per cent may not care about the poor, the environment or preserving local character. It can manipulate populations through social media, replace human jobs with robots and undermine democracy. In reaction to this has been a resurgence of localism. This can take many forms both good (civic and environmental responsibility) and bad (nationalism and racism). Berwick can be a parable of Borderlands spirituality where both the local and the global have their rightful place.

My Berwick house is a blessing. As a quid pro quo for me leasing my Lindisfarne house to the Community for £1 per year, the Community put out an appeal for donations and loans and purchased a restored Georgian terraced house at 7 Wallace Green for my use. Locals dispute the reason it is named Wallace Green. One version is that William Wallace (the hero of the film *Braveheart*) was imprisoned in the building opposite me (a former prison) before being taken to the Tower of London to be executed.

The house feels right for its purpose. It comprises an office/prayer room, bedroom, guest room, lounge/meeting room, kitchen and a walled back yard. I have loved gardens throughout my life. At Westfield Avenue I was given a rectangular patch. I bordered it with stones and planted flowers and a few vegetables in it. In London, Stoke-on-Trent and at first on Holy Island I had virtually no garden. Until I acquired the White House, which had one of the most beautiful gardens on the island. It was hard work but a delight. I created a vegetable patch at the bottom. To maintain such a garden was beyond my powers in old age, so I was grateful that the community's house which I tenanted at Berwick had this small back yard. I knew that this, too, must be adorned with the beauty of flowers, the scents that would attract bees, and the herbs that could grace meals. I also attracted birds. This patio, bedecked with plant pots, the crevices in its historic walls filled with creepers, is to me a foretaste of heaven. Berwick Rail Station has a sign 'Berwick: for Holy Island'; I named my new home Lindisfarne Links and my sister gave me a metal wild goose which hangs on my patio wall pointing towards Lindisfarne. So I am in a Borderland that embraces Holy Island.

At one level I like Berwick. People greet you. Within a minute I can walk into the Church of Scotland, the Salvation Army, the Roman Catholic hall or the Church of England; there a few of us say Morning Prayer from our iPhones at 8.30 a.m. each morning. This, the church I now belong to, Holy Trinity Berwick, is the northernmost C of E church in England, and one of only two built by Cromwell, hence it has no steeple.

As the climate crisis looms large, and as COVID-19 spread, the concept of the 'twenty-minute neighbourhood' took off. Hatched in Melbourne and adopted in England's Waltham Forest, the idea is that shops, schools, parks and all key facilities are within a twenty minute walk, cycle or bus ride, thus pushing cars to the margins. In Berwick the shops and the medical facilities take two minutes, the rail station twelve. Nearby educational, history, fitness, music and civic networks flourish – though there are too few job opportunities and too many depressed people.

Unlike most of humanity, I have lived my life in a different borderland – between wars. I doubt this can last much longer. Huge numbers even of the world's present citizens have suffered war, holocaust and refugee camps. My life has been a privilege that I must use to the full.

More widely, the word Borderland indicates a spirituality that is the opposite of the closed in. It refers to borderlands between one place or one season and another, between the familiar and the unknown, between the everyday and the eternal. In his book *Borderlands* David Adam writes: 'Somehow the Celtic peoples, due to their history, have been able to keep an awareness of the "other" far more easily than most peoples ... Everything spoke of a Presence, vibrated with his love. They saw a universe ablaze with His glory, suffused with a presence that calls, nods and beckons ... Such an awareness has us always treading exciting border lands.' In his book *Living Between Worlds* Philip Sheldrake points out that Celtic Christians have a strong sense of living in boundary places between the material world and the other world. The surrounding physical world is both a concrete reality and a doorway into another, spiritual world.

So, towards the end of my life, I started to tread border lands. On my soul friend's advice, I entered a season of reflection on making transitions. It is hard to let go of one's own baby. If one does succeed in letting go the matter does not end there. When God calls a person to guard the ethos of a community it is implanted in the soul until death, and possibly beyond death: that does not change. What changes is that the worldly, organizational means of doing that are no longer available. It must be done through prayer, relationship, listening to God and appropriately sharing what one hears. That requires spiritual intelligence.

I came late to *The Twenty One Skills of Spiritual Intelligence* by Cindy Wigglesworth. It is one of the most transforming books I have read. I realized that I had spent much of my life trying to serve God like a clumsy elephant. She defines spiritual intelligence as 'the ability to be aware of one's own and others' frames of reference while operating from a center of empathy and compassion, and maintaining inner and outer peace regardless of the situation'. I worked to integrate those skills that I had previously lacked. I continued to carry the dispersed community in my heart and to share in a fellowship of love but sought to pursue only those actions that were spiritually intelligent.

Healing the wounds

The transition from Holy Island was difficult. Countering the practical and psychological reasons for leaving was my inner narrative that God had called me to lay down my life for the island, for better or worse until death parted us. This narrative was buttressed by letters from Christians who said it was the devil's plan that I should leave, and that opposition was a sign that we were doing God's will.

If you are a mis-represented participant in a toxic situation do you: a) protest?; b) keep silent?; c) run away?; d) become ill or paralysed by emotional pain?; e) humbly submit like a lamb to the slaughter?; f) pretend things did not happen?; g) shake the dust off your feet?; or h) smugly remind people that saints like Teresa of Avila, John of the Cross and John Wesley were treated like that? I did all of those things. Then I realized I was in danger of becoming a Pharisee. I must learn to look at this story from the perspective of my Shadow.

I have worked on befriending my Shadow for a quarter of a century. In my skimpy meetings with First Nation peoples I came to realise the truth broadcast by a Queensland Aboriginal Activists Group: 'If you have come to help me you are wasting our time. But if you come because your liberation is bound up with mine, then let us work together.' When I listen to my Shadow I now know that this holds true for fellow residents too.

At the age of 78 I read in Ruth Haley Barton's *Strengthening the Soul of Your Leadership*: 'A leader who experienced not being wanted at conception or birth learns to doubt his basic self-worth and develops patterns of hiding his real self from others. This type of leader remains distant or aloof because that seems easier than risking more rejection. It prevents him from entering into authentic community, which is essential to spiritual leadership.' On p. 77 Ruth Haley Barton describes our existential angst:

> Our calling is woven into the fabric of our being. It encompasses everything that makes us who we are: our genetics, innate orientations and capacities, our personality,

heredity and life-shaping experiences, and the time and place into which we were born. Vocation comes from a voice inside calling me to be the person I was born to be, to fulfil the original self, given to me at birth by God. But by the time we know there is such a thing as the true self, the false self has taken over. There is a huge gulf between our true self and the designs and plans that the ego has for us. The complicated art of vocation discernment lies in untangling these threads.

I confessed to my soul friend that, despite so many 'God moments', much of my life was still determined by my self-centered and wounded 'childhood script'. How could this ever change? Peter suggested I find an alternative script. 'What could that be?' I disbelievingly retorted. 'Agape?' he wondered. Agape, the endless flow of unconditional compassion from God's heart offered to me. At first I thought this was impossible, but then my Protestant pedigree came into play. Martin Luther had taught that we are put right with God (justified) by faith. Faith means I act as if something has happened. Whenever I felt the childhood script dictating my responses, by faith I claimed Agape as my greater script. God is changing me.

When I moved out of Holy Island I tried to let go of my hopes and dreams, daily repeating the Scripture verse, 'Unless a grain of wheat falls into the ground and dies it cannot bear fruit' (John 12:24). I learned to become fully present to new friends in Berwick – or so I thought – until two things brought me up sharp. I met a Norwegian church leader friend who had worked through his anger with a psychotherapist for a year after having to leave a church which deeply hurt him. He quizzed me about Lindisfarne and asked, 'What have you done with your anger?' 'I have parked it', I replied. 'That is no answer – you need to see a psychotherapist', he said.

Then I got what I thought was bad toothache. But the dentist, after she had taken photographs, informed me that I did not have toothache, I had jaw ache. I was gnashing my teeth at night so much that the muscles on the jaw had become damaged. This alerted me to the fact that anger was harming me. I began to pay attention to it. It was anger at thwarted vocation, both mine and more widely the community's vocation to contribute to a recovery of the lived spirituality that Aidan first patterned on Lindisfarne. At first, I felt anger towards certain elements. But after talking this through with a therapist he suggested that some of this anger was with myself. Paulo Coelho points out that haters don't really hate you, they hate themselves because you are a reflection of what they wish to be. So the task of people like me is to help these neighbours find their greatness.

Even while I was busy taking Sunday services in outlying churches, networking internationally and doing creative writing, I had bad dreams. One nightmare was so horrific I shared it with spiritual companions and then with a Jungian analyst. It featured a teenager I knew. His body was horribly deformed and almost disconnected from his head, part of which was missing. Both his body and head had to be covered in shawls, so ghastly were they to look upon. Yet from his eyes radiated joy and compassion for all. Jungians say dreams are almost always about the dreamer. So I interpreted the dream as a representation of my repressed emotional make-up. My life calling had almost been destroyed (or recent opposition had revealed the damaged infant still in the womb of the soul) but if Jesus lit my eyes, then the entire body might again become whole (Luke 11:34). Was this a last-chance hint that healing was still possible? A friend suggested I ask Jesus to hold my neck and join my body and head together. The Jungian analyst, however, to my astonishment, suggested the dream could be about the wound in the Body of Christ. If this were the case, I must no longer relate to critics as a hurt refugee, but as a potential healer, with understanding, and without judgement. Now, as a I re-live this dream, I see fresh flesh growing on that horrific body. Soon, the coverings can come off.

Gratitude now competes with self-pity as my dominant emotion. I am grateful for all that my sister gives. I am grateful that CAH guardians, Caim Council and area groups in UK and elsewhere show such integrity and dedication.

Another factor in inner healing is clearing up confusion. My soul friend helped me to see that I had been accountable to the Church of England, but some people in the institution had confused my need to be accountable with their need to control. They did not like the fact that I had been released by the Church of England to work across denominations and geographical boundaries. Like John Wesley 'the world was my parish'. John Wesley was once estranged but is now embraced by the Church of England. 'You can be at peace about this' they said.

Another factor in healing is wounded group memory. One element in Holy Island's 'difficulties' is centuries old. Some people believe that island memory has been wounded since the time of the Benedictine Priory, whose monks seem to have reflected the feudal class system in their attitude to islanders. I suppose it would have been regarded as an extension of French/Norman rule in these islands. Roland Walls, the hermit founder of The Community of the Resurrection near Edinburgh, who was for a time spiritual director to Holy Island's Marygate Retreat House, warned that the idea that the islanders were low class people who had to doff their hats to the high class people who ran the church had permeated the psyche of the islanders, even though the Benedictines had been dissolved five hundred years ago and modern church people might well be as poor as the rest. So we invite people to pray for on-going healing of submerged group memory.

Moving on

A pilgrim asked, 'What is the purpose of growing old?' A retreatant replied, 'To make space for others to grow.' Ruth Booth, who had been a church warden at St Mary's for three years was soon to retire as a doctor north of the Border. Now, after ten years on the island, she and Graham decided to leave. They received a remarkable new call, but this was a sad loss for the island. At 11.00 a.m. one morning Graham realised that he could see an image of the premises of the Society of Our Lady of the Isles on Fetlar, in Shetland, as if it were projected on the wall above his computer. He had visited there 15 years previously but had had no contact with Mother Mary Agnes since then. He felt called to pray for the sisters and stopped work to do so. After praying again later in the day with Ruth he expected to quietly get on with life on Lindisfarne. However, the following day he could still see the image and, after trying to contact the sisters, phoned the Society's warden the Very Revd Gerald Stranraer-Mull. Their conversation revealed that at 11.00 a.m. the previous day Mother Mary Agnes's trustees, chaired by the Bishop of Aberdeen, had decided to put their monastic-style buildings on Fetlar up for sale. Weeks later, after a long conversation with Mother Mary Agnes, Graham and Ruth agreed to visit Fetlar for a period of discernment as to whether God was calling them to buy the properties and move north. After some days on both Unst and Fetlar, and after carefully praying, measuring and envisioning, they decided that these properties were not right for them, but instead, through a remarkable set of 'coincidences' they met the owners of the old West Manse at Tresta Bay who had that day decided to sell up and move south. Six months later Graham and Ruth purchased this house with its grounds and outbuildings, moved to Fetlar and began the long process of rebuilding and turning it not only into their home but into a Quiet House of Prayer and Retreat. When the SOLI premises were eventually sold and the chapel de-consecrated, they were part of the ending of that season and of the 'handing on of the baton of prayer', receiving the Celtic Cross from the SOLI chapel from Mother Mary Agnes and the Bishop of Aberdeen and Orkney. They continue a daily pattern of prayer in their own chapel and enjoy a close friendship with the sisters, and their house has become a ministry of special blessing.

I was sad to miss their farewell since I was in Cyprus. So I wrote this blessing which was given to them on a beautiful, framed picture by Mary Fleeson of Lindisfarne Scriptorium:

Blessing of memory be yours – of heaven opening gates in
pilgrim hearts
Blessing of journey be yours – companioning others in
their sorrows
Blessing of homestead be yours – its gravel bejewelled by God.

Carol Few, the Secretary of the dispersed Community, received her pension lump sum and also moved from Holy Island to Berwick.

Following a short-lived appointment of Open Gate wardens during which time I moved to Berwick, Whitehouse became vacant again, though volunteers often stayed there. Many were delighted when three island residents were invited to staff the Open Gate – each had talent, empathy and was well-liked. At first none were church-goers, but all were spiritual. Kayleah became the house manager, Jutta the catering manager, and Robert the site manager. Kayleah's grandmother, Dorothy, lives on the island.

They worked as a community of equals. Before the COVID pandemic I routinely spent one day a week on the island when I took Midday Prayer and talked with them. On average I spend another day each week with individuals or groups who wish to talk or have spiritual direction.

The Open Gate hosted a memorable celebration of my 80th birthday in March 2020, to which friends and relatives came from far parts of the UK. It was just in time. The COVID-19 pandemic spread across the world and caused shut-down shortly afterwards. Like millions of others I was isolated in my house. We new monastics are familiar with the 'Cave, Refectory, Road' pattern. I embraced this with the help of The Five P's: 1) Projects (my project was to complete the Year Book *Re-Imagining the British Isles with Ireland*; 2) Prayer Pauses morning, noon and night; 3) Persons (I rang, emailed or chatted outside the front door to one or two folk each day); 4) Physicals (inspired by 'the nation's PE teacher Joe Wicks and weights, plus one or two walks along the River Tweed or the coast, up 100 steps, etc.); 5) Perusals (reading, viewing or journalling).

Retreats at Open Gate were cancelled but twice as many booked for on-line versions. It dawned on me that the new monasticism has been put in place for this new epoch. The initial vehicle is not the vision. The COVID-19 pandemic caused many retreat houses to close and, as I write, it looks as if ours may be among them. The Divine Pruner is at work (John 15:2). At midnight on new Year's Night 2021 I climbed to a high point that looks over Holy Island and recited this prayer: 'As tides recede, we plant fresh steps in the sand, as white flakes fall we plant fresh steps in the snow, as a new year dawns we plant fresh virtues in our lands.'

As the landlord of Whitehouse I sometimes helped other volunteers with the garden. I was willing to gift it to the community in my will on condition that the community sustained the Celtic Christianity Library and used Whitehouse to facilitate the original vision for CAH on Holy Island, which included facilitating placements and resourcing church leaders. I had the following words framed:

Whitehouse

Martin of Tours' fourth-century White House at Liguges, which combined the contemplative life with evangelism and social care, became a prototype that spread throughout Gaul to Celtic lands. Ninian established a white house at Whithorn, which was a mother house to small white houses established in each mission area. These embraced the current Scottish shires of Ayr, Glasgow, Forfar, Aberdeen, Inverness, Sutherland, right up to the Orkney Islands. Welsh Christian leaders took this model back from Whithorn to their home areas. They became spiritual hearths in what is now Wales. It is thought that White Houses stretched from Dornoch in the north of Pictland to Ty Gwyn ar Dav in Wales. Ty Gwyn (Welsh for 'White' or 'Blessed House'), near Whitesands Bay in Pembrokeshire, is a former monastic site with ties to Saints Patrick and David. Other Welsh places named Ty Gwyn include the supposed site of the legendary Welsh parliament that produced the Laws of Hywel Dda, Whitland in Carmarthenshire, and Tygwyn railway station at Glan-y-wern in Gwynedd on the Cambrian Line. The Pict Ternan, who later became abbot of Whithorn, was baptised by one of Ninian's elderly helpers, Paul the Aged. Despite his age, Paul went on to found his own White House by the river Davi in Carmarthenshire. Both Paul the Aged and Manchan (the Little Monk), Ternan's successor as Whithorn's abbot, taught David (Wales' patron saint), who later founded his community at Menevia.

Pray God this Whitehouse fans this tradition into flame today.

My good friend Scott Brennan has an outstanding ministry as a church planter and as a mentor of emerging church leaders. He has developed The Lighthouse church, an embryo 'village of God' at Prestonpans. The Church of Scotland, the Episcopal, Baptist and other churches have used him in their training programmes. He and his talented wife Faith, who also exercises leadership gifts, looked to have a base from which they can transition from hands-on leadership to mentoring a new generation. They have long followed the Way of Life. Following extensive discussions the community agreed that from March 2021 they would live in Whitehouse, and use it as a base for a ministry to emerging church leaders and student placements.

I drew up a list of every house on Holy Island and started to pray for each person. I then left everything to God.

Then the coronavirus epidemic closed the island down. Businesses and charities alike suffered greatly and the Community is having to make hard decisions. In the *Holy Island Times* I likened the second lockdown in England to a winter womb. It is dark and bleak, yet new birthings can come as they did at the first Christmas. In September 2020, during a break in the Covid epidemic, someone wrote these lines on Holy Island:

Island of Light, Island of hope, Island of Birthings.
Birthings of seeds sown long ago,
Cuthbert in prayer, Aidan's Community of light and life …
As the world struggles in pain with fear and with questions,
You are here in this place!
New Life in Your Kingdom is being birthed.
Hope is being re kindled,
Light is shining through the darkness.
Your Spirit is dancing in the shadows ready to reveal new ways,
New possibilities,
New horizons of promise.
Seeds of prayers sown long ago take root and grow,

A harvest yet to be revealed,
In Your time,
In your way,
In Your moments yet to be.

Jean Kirkpatrick

Old-age activities

Some fifteen churches in the hinterland of several deaneries were at various times without a resident priest, so I enjoyed being on a rota, visiting these churches, conducting Eucharists, preaching and befriending the gathered local faithful. It is hard work. Lowick at 9.00 a.m., Etal at 10.30 a.m. and Ancroft at 12.00 leaves me exhausted though fulfilled. But what a privilege to celebrate Christmas Day with the angels at St Aidan's Church, Bamburgh – perhaps the same angels who escorted Aidan to heaven in that place; or to become friends with the lively congregation at St Ebbe's, Beadnell. They know Ebbe as the Mother of Northumbria. Once a year they have an open air service by the ruins of her monastery on St Ebbe's Nook. I could name so many Northumberland treasures of architecture, history and faithful Christian community that I have briefly served on a Sunday.

Each church has different habits, so I compiled a *Dummies Guide to Sunday Services for Itinerant Worship Leaders*. Here are just a few items:

> Before leaving home write down: the names and contact details of the church wardens, organist, readers, etc.; allow ten extra minutes when the Sat Nav has never heard of the church. In case the church does not provide the form of service, print out your own; if the church uses the 1662 Book of Common Prayer, cross out 'king' and replace with 'queen', etc., etc. Do I count the number of people and therefore of wafers for the Communion service (during a hymn?) If not, who will tell me the numbers? Do I lead the prayers or someone else? Note that on the third Sunday it's the Brown family but not if their boy is in a bad mood. If it's me, ask someone who needs

prayer. How many steps are there at each end of the altar? (Look down.) Sign the register and include the number of worshippers. If, as is usual, neither church has a toilet, check a suitable group of bushes behind which to relieve oneself (if male) or a suitable, open and friendly public house (if a woman) unless she is an equal rights for women crusader; e.g. three miles after the farm, two bends in the road, stop at track and relieve yourself behind the second group of bushes … If the church is locked, wait until start time and go home: I am absolved of all responsibility.

Of course, during the COVID lockdown the ecclesiastical powers-that-be ruled that nobody over seventy should normally risk taking any services.

It is an easy walk to Berwick railway station. In the November of my first year there I spent a month in Birmingham with Geoff and Joy Holt, at their CAH house named The Cairn, which flows with hospitality. There I dialogued with a variety of Muslim evangelists who have stalls in the marketplace, and had conversations with inter-faith clergy. I spent time at St Chad's Well near Lichfield Cathedral and experienced the Holt's sterling work with the Narthex Food and Clothes Bank project. I drafted a little book entitled 'Letters to Muslims', but if I want to stay alive it might be wise to publish it the day I die.

I also maintained contacts with Ash Barker and friends who, following years living in Bangkok slums, developed in his revolutionary new ministry at Newbigin House, Birmingham, near the prison. He leads a Fresh Expression of Church in a yurt in the garden. His wife Anji heads up the multiple activities of Newbigin Community Trust, and they oversee the School for Urban Leadership. He invited me back to give a Celtic blessing on the yurt. This was it:

> May each person who enters this yurt
> Receive from You a big spurt
> To fight for right and overcome wrong
> To laugh and dance and sing your song.

Teach us to number our days

A group of ancients meet for a monthly pub chat. One of us can't believe in anything for which there is no scientific evidence such as God, or life after death.

In 2018 I joined the Haddington Serious Book Club. This mainly consists of a Jesuit and Presbyterian theologians. In 2019 our first selected book was *Waiting for the Last Bus: Reflections on Life and Death* by Richard Holloway, a former Episcopal Bishop of Edinburgh and now a wobbly agnostic. He repeats novelist Julian Barnes' four categories of human approaches to death: those who do not fear death because they have faith and those who do not fear it despite having no faith; those who despite having faith can't rid themselves of visceral fear of death, and those who fear death and have no faith. Holloway falls into the second category. I realized that I fell into the third. I do sometimes wonder, along with selfless and noble Buddhists, how much of our belief in an afterlife is a projection of our selfish egos. I read The Tibetan Book of Living and Dying and practised discarding all attachments, even attachments to a life after death made in my own image.

Life is a bet. I have bet my life on God. What if God does not exist? Stephen Hawking thinks there is no need for a God hypothesis to explain the Big Bang and the laws of the cosmos. As I have opened myself to impressions of The Beyond in the Midst, to Love behind love, I have received impulses of love that have qualities of grace, givenness, and that lead to fulfilling outcomes. I suppose this could be reduced to a law of synchronicity, of reaping what we sow, in this life only, but it takes some explaining. Also, it seems to me that the evidence that Jesus Christ rose from the dead is very strong, and that the words imputed to him in the Gospels are in essence authentic.

The phrase 'teach us to number our days' comes from the Bible (Psalm 90:12), so some years ago I started to number my days. I multiplied the number of days in a year by the number of years I had lived. I reckoned I had lived 24,660 days. Then I did a newspaper quiz that claimed the reader could calculate the age they would most likely die. This was based on parents' longevity, and one's health and life-style. I discovered that I would die when I was eighty-four years and three months. I translated this into the number of days. Blithely disregarding God's rebuke of King David for gathering unnecessary statistics, I posted on my bedroom door the number of days I had left to live. Each day I ticked another one off. The moral is: each day is important; offer it to God and live it to the full. Then I heard that the new old age is 85-95 and gave up counting the days.

Of course, God may know better than we. 'I suffer from the Methuselah tendency', a very old friend informed me in a card. I began to investigate this tendency. I learned that Methuselah had a family of long-livers who became elders to the people who lived in the time before Noah. His father was Enoch, the great-grandfather of Noah. Enoch is the subject of early Jewish, Christian, and Muslim writings. The Bible says that Enoch lived 365 years and that he walked with God before 'God took him'. Enoch's life certainly caught God's attention, and it catches mine, too. He is mentioned in the New Testament as one of the great people of faith (Hebrews 11:5). Church Fathers, like St John of Damascus, and some modern Evangelical commentators, consider Enoch to be one of the Two Witnesses in the Book of Revelation. They are like two olive trees, producing much oil which flows continually into the lampstands which keep God's kingdom lit up. With that template before me I resolved to keep walking until God took me.

As a student I was moved to learn that Pope John XXIII had, each Lent since he himself was a student, meditated as if he was on his death bed. This helped him to jettison trivial pursuits and focus on what is eternally significant. I have long meditated in this way. I also grew to admire champion martial arts and swords persons. One novice was told by his sword master, 'You are already a champion because you have no fear of death.' That is why the theme of my book *Before We Say Goodbye* is that in order to die well we have to live well. As I prepare to lead a retreat on Dying Well, I place by my bed things I may need as Last Passage aids: recordings of music, copies of prayers, texts of Scripture such as 'I am the Resurrection and the Life … I will come to you that where I am there you may be'; a picture of the Rainbow beams radiating from

Christ's Sacred Heart and a photo of the rose window in Berwick Parish Church at the heart of which is The Lamb Slain before the Foundation of the World – the Eternal Pity – Defenceless Love – in the heart of the Omega, the ultimate and endless Completer of all.

Berwick has over one hundred resident swans who are faithful for life. The word swansong comes from the myth that swans sing when they die. One Berwick local swears they heard a dying swan sing. So I pondered what my swansong might be. Maybe it will be that chorus I learned as a teenager: 'Moment by moment I'm kept in his love, moment by moment I've life from above. Looking to Jesus till glory shall shine, moment by moment, O Lord, I am thine.'

Priest

As I engage with the on-going British-Irish reconciliation process and realise the harm the Church of England's monarchical governors have inflicted upon Ireland, I can no longer approve of my membership of the Church of England. This church has been yoked to oppressive colonial power. The monarch imposed English clergy upon Ireland and Scotland in order to thwart the will of their peoples. The oath of allegiance still required before any person can be ordained into the Church of England is, 'I, A B, do swear that I will be faithful and bear true allegiance to Her Majesty Queen Elizabeth II, her heirs and successors, according to law...' I need to be free to fight to change bad laws. Christ is not only head of the church as Calvinists teach, he is King of kings.

On the other hand I am appalled at the ignorance of many evangelicals and Roman Catholics as to the roots of the Church of England. Unlike churches on the continent, who when they split from Rome started new churches with no inherited bonds with the universal church, many churches in England continued as they were before, in some cases with the same parish priests and bishops, and with the concept of 'the apostolic succession'. Hence the dictum that the Church of England is both Catholic and Reformed. A Roman Catholic visitor to St Mary's Holy Island spoke to me in front of the votive candle stand filled with lighted candles, while I was on duty. 'Is this church Catholic or Protestant?', he asked. My answer in full was: 'I was ordained at the Lichfield Cathedral founded in the seventh century by Lindisfarne's Saint Chad into the One, Holy, Catholic and Apostolic Church.' I remain deeply grateful for this.

However, I have grown increasingly aware that Christianity has two lungs, the western rational lung and the eastern mystical lung. I now draw much from the Eastern Orthodox lung. Incense and ikons adorn my chapel and I devour books by Orthodox monks. When I shared in the Celtic Orthodox Church colloquium at Saint Dol, a Swiss Bishop told me I had an Orthodox spirit and he would be happy to ordain me as an Orthodox. When I said I would first have to ask my Diocesan Bishop he said, 'No, no, no, Mr Simpson, this is just between us.' Only commitment to transparency caused me to resist this temptation. I often bear in mind the words spoken to me by a monk in Cyprus: 'If you bring to me members of the Church of England who show the same fruits as the desert fathers and the fathers here – then I will accept it as a true church.'

Because Catholics, Episcopal/Anglicans, Orthodox, Lutherans/ Protestants, Quakers, Pentecostals and friends of Jesus from other faith traditions follow the CAH Way of Life, and my role is to affirm them, I have held back from dwelling on my personal tradition, because I see it as provisional. If I were a Turk I would be an Orthodox, if I were an Italian I would be a Catholic, if I were a Middle Easterner I would be an Oriental, if I were a Scandinavian I would be a Lutheran, and since I am British I am part of the Episcopal/Anglican family – but in each case with a conscience clause. If I had my time again I would be happy to be ordained in any province of the Episcopal Communion outside of England, for they do not require an oath of allegiance to the Sovereign of England.

Nevertheless I am deeply impressed by the insights into monarchy by the makers of the Netflix series *The Crown* – that monarchy is a calling of God to hold the elected rulers to reflect God's will. I would even make an oath to the English monarch with the additional phrase 'inasmuch as he upholds God's laws'.

Tell your story

As I look back, I feel wistful about the funerals I conducted for some poor person who went out in a box apparently never having lived. They had no friends, merely the statutory representative of Social Services, a funeral director and a priest. They had just existed. I recall a grave-digger I sat next to in a Toronto pub. 'My greatest sadness,' he confided in me, 'is to see so many people being lowered to their grave who have never told their story.' So as my memory fades, I complete my autobiography before I forget the story. Revelation 20:12 refers to God's books in which are written the deeds of all who have died. If God writes books about our lives, and we are made to reflect God, it seems a good thing to do. It is a finishing touch which helps me to be grateful for God's leading. It may also furnish the memory of loved ones left behind.

Comparing a leader's life to that of Moses, Ruth Haley Barton suggests that we turn aside into desert contemplation until we become aware of the burning bush. In order to discern the golden thread of God's calling we do well to list the burning bush experiences in our lives – the moments when God's impulses have filled the spaces we have created. I began to work on this autobiography with that end in view.

I recalled Sir John Laing's call to me as a school leaver to live the rest of my life like a candle that steadily burns until everything has been used up in God's service. I recalled Russ Parker likening me, at the genesis of the Community of Aidan and Hilda, to the fire that burned in the prophet Jeremiah: 'But if I say, 'I will not mention his word or speak anymore in his name, his word is in my heart like a fire, a fire shut up in my bones. I am weary of holding it in; indeed, I cannot' (Jeremiah 20:9). I recalled the countless times when I simply had to speak or write because of this fire. Although at times in my life I raged or rambled, although I stumbled from prison to prism, nevertheless one season unfolded into another, the frail water of life flossed round another corner, an ember fanned into a flame.

The word calling is surely linked to the verb to call: I burn to call out or communicate something eternally important and currently timely that is like a fire. This calling is so divine that I must suffer the fires that burn out false patterns, born of willfulness and fear and pre-conceived constructs, and yet orient my life towards realities that others do not see. What I have come to realise is that most of my life I have sought God to show me what I should do: now I must ask God to show me how to love.

The next thousand years

The last thing on my Bucket List had been the pilgrimage to the Ecumenical Patriarch. If God spared me, I thought, I might return to a Coptic monastery or to Mount Sinai, but that was it. Then came the biggest finishing touch one can imagine: 'Put something in place for the next thousand years.' It came about like this.

When the Community of Aidan and Hilda was launched, a sister at the Community of All Hallows (CAH) on the Norfolk/ Suffolk border stated that our Way of Life would have long term significance. In 2019 I recalled David Adam's vision for an SAS and I wrote down: 'The Community of Aidan and Hilda is God's SAS for the next thousand years. Raise up people who are real, rooted, and rhythmic. Who will raise the next generation? Who will recruit and mentor Joshuas? Who will reach Africans with something more lasting than the Prosperity Gospel? Who will connect with indigenous peoples? The urgent crowds out the eternal. The short-term crowds out the long-term.'

In 1987 the philosopher Alasdair MacIntyre painted a bleak picture of trends in the American way of life, which he thought might lead to a new Dark Age and called for 'a new Benedict' – though he thought this new type of monastic would be unlike the first. This has led to fresh thinking, publicized in books such as *The Benedict Option* in 2017. In this book conservative columnist Rod Dreher calls on American Christians to prepare for the coming Dark Age by embracing an ancient Christian way of life.

I am convinced that Benedict is the wrong ikon for our future. Writing of terrible abuse in prestigious English Benedictine schools *The Tablet* of 18 August 2018 concluded: 'The problems go even deeper than the particular problems of English Benedictines – as far as the sixth century rule of St Benedict, by which the monks live. Benedict's rule reflects a patriarchal theology in which belief in an all-knowing, all-powerful God the Father is mirrored in an all-powerful male leader. This gives huge authority to the abbot – an authority which some of them have been unwilling to surrender to the police or social services, or even allow them to challenge their views or decisions.' When people feel that 'things fall apart, the centre cannot hold' (Yeats) it is understandable that they want to create some protected 'zones of stability'. But if God is in the falling apart, might he not want leaders to abandon themselves to the process, and use tools that help them to navigate the ocean of flux without hitting the reefs? The Irish 'pilgrims for the love of God' who travelled across the continent did more to re-evangelise Dark Age Europe than the top down missions or stay-put monasteries. The model we need is a Celtic new monasticism which lets God be our inner compass so that we can navigate the third millennium seas.

I believe that one reason why Benedictinism survived a thousand years is that Benedict wrote 73 short chapters of commentary on how to live the Rule in given circumstances. If our Way of Life were to contribute to a foundation that would last a thousand years it needed, I concluded, a detailed commentary. It could be on a take it or leave it basis, but for those who wished, it could be the basis of a life-long spiritual formation. As a prelude to this I worked night and day on an on-line email course. This consists of an email each day on alternate weeks for four years. Every seventh email provides resources and reflective exercises. One of our Australian Guardians, Bruce Challenor, expended enormous time and energy pasting each one of these on to MailChimp. People can enrol on www.waymarksoflife.com.

I said to Brent Lyons-Lee, 'How do we get millennials to enrol?' He replied 'If you want to enlist millennials you need an App'. This seemed too huge a challenge at my age – I have no expertise in IT, App-making or marketing. Until my friend Scott Brennan said, 'Do you remember Graeme who prophesied over you when you came to our Lighthouse church? He has just finished uni and has set up an App-making business. In May he will marry Laura who hopes to start a marketing business. Get in touch with them.' Graeme prophesied over me again. 'You are a Caleb. He was as strong at eighty-five as when God first called him and was ready for whatever new service God had for him in the new land they had come to'. Even if only a bit of that applied to me, I set myself to the task. Within six months I had completed the text, Bible readings, prayers, reflections, resources and picture suggestions for about 180 days. Now Graeme had to get artists and produce the final product, we had to crowd fund and do marketing.

Someone said, 'The Community of Aidan and Hilda needs to be a place around which a fallen civilization can reform'. For decades I have alerted churchgoers to the fact that the Christendom the West has known for the last 1500 years is dying. Contemporary analysts peer into the future. Algorithms have re-fuelled fascism, the dissolution of the social contract that underpins democracies, and the end of trans-national peace partnerships. An unholy alliance between the arrogant rich and the angry poor has brainwashed electorates. Artificial Intelligence looks likely to do away with human jobs. Stephen Hawking thought that AI could spell the end of the human race.

Christianity is just one ball being kicked around with a hundred other balls –the balls of fashion and fortune, righteous indignation and Buddhist resignation. People turn off Jesus because he is associated with the manipulative institutions of the West. Jesus needs to be re-born. We are in the twilight of western dominance. The new China Belt Road, which travels through more than 70 countries, is the equivalent of the roads of the Roman Empire. Already Chinese workers in African countries are becoming Followers of the Way. The matrix consists of dying and defenceless love, a movement that spread like mushrooms among the slave classes of the Roman Empire, a movement that is reborn in the womb of the third millennium named after Him.

Church leaders from other lands contacted me. How did I see an emerging post-COVID society? Scientists have found evidence of the disappearance of wildlife at an accelerating rate, prompting fears of a sixth mass extinction that will endanger human survival.

The European empires have become inglorious, in part through Black Lives Matter's bringing mass awareness of the evil of the slave trade. The USA empire is revealed as capitalism ('money is God') dressed up in the name of the Bible.

So now I work on the Commentary on the Way of Life that, if it pleases God, will last a thousand years. It breaks down our Way of Life and our Constitution into fifty two chapters – one for each week of the year. It includes a Psalm, an Old Testament and a New Testament reading for each day of each week. It is succinct – it seeks to express in memorable words the core of this way. It will take time to complete, but its final words are already drafted: 'The world as we know it may be destroyed by holocaust or climate damage. The arena of God's experiment on earth may shift to Oceania and China, but wherever people follow this Way, there Christ's Presence will be.'

Finishing touches

What are the finishing touches God wants to work in me? I am an Enneagram Type 4. Its imprints loom large in this selective autobiography. Type 4s are always apologising. Sorry. In contrast, as I recall from a Kate Tristram sermon in my book St Aidan's Way of Mission in which she said of Aidan, 'There was a man who seemed to his friends to be all gift – no threat', I asked myself, 'Can my life be a gift to the world every day, including my last day?'

At the Community's annual gathering on Zoom our Members' Guardian, Penny Warren, said: 'When we look with only one eye, we see without depth. When we look only at life and success and good things, we see without depth. In this time of fear, anxiety, loneliness and grief in the pandemic I think it is as though the other eye has been opened, the eye that sees death and frailty and looks them in the face. Now we see with both eyes and we see with greater depth.' As I reflected on the 'eye of the eagle' some words came back to me from our Caim retreat the previous spring when Simon (Reed) shared these words: The years of preparations are done. You have been schooled in my ways at the feet of the saints.

Now is the time to go with the book and the bell into the wild hills and the pagan places. There are many places of resurrection, it is your call to find them.'

Could the shut-down isolation of the COVID-19 pandemic become a liminal space that bridges earth and heaven in which we find our place of resurrection? The idea of a passive eternity bores me. Jesus' promises seem to me to envisage a resurrected life of the real me. I am still in the process of compiling Scripture verses that give hints as to what heaven might be like. The Bible speaks of a new space and a new earth. If Jesus promised his apostles that after death they would be given responsibility for a tribe, and there are innumerable tribes, I guess I may be given responsibility for something. After all, Jesus implied that if we have been faithful with our earthly work opportunities, we will be entrusted with eternal work opportunities, Luke 16:11. Before Jesus left this earth he prayed 'Father, I desire that those you have given me may be with me where I am, to see my glory, which you have given me before the foundation of the world' (John 17:24). Jesus said his Father had never stopped working and neither had he, so I presume being with him implies that we share in the work.

We will first have to disintegrate. That is not a pleasant process. The Christian doctrine of the resurrection of the body implies to me that there will be a speeded-up re-constitution of our disintegrated elements. The Book of Revelation speaks of Christ as the Alpha and the Omega, the Originator and the ultimate Fulfiller. Quantum physics suggests that when you break down matter to its core it is more like an essence, and these essences change according to the way they are perceived. If you talk nicely to plants they are more likely to do well. If we are loved, we are more likely to respond in love. If God is not just Alpha (the Big Bang and all that) but also the Omega, every little bit of the cosmos can be loved into existence and loved out of malformation. The Omega – the fulfilment of all things – will perceive us with infinite love. We will flourish beyond our earthly imaginings. Our God-given uniqueness will not be extinguished – we will joy in the oneness of self-aware souls with the One who fills all.

The Orthodox not only sanctify death, they sanctify the disintegration that precedes it. In my flesh I do not relish disintegration, but if some part of The Way of Life has sunk into the soil of humanity and added to the soul of the cosmos, I shall joyfully traverse this crossing place into the way that lasts for ever.

Books and Resources from Ray Simpson

For Ray's weekly blogs, free downloads and details of his forty books, DVD or MP3 visit www.raysimpson.org.

His three most recent most books are:
   Celtic Christianity and Climate Crisis: Twelve Keys for the Future of the Church (Sacristy Press).
   Hilda of Whitby: A Spirituality of Now (BRF)
   Aidan of Lindisfarne: Irish Flame Warms a New World (Wipf & Stock) (a historical novel).
His best-selling book of worship material is *Liturgies from Lindisfarne* (Mayhew Publishing).
His three books on new monasticism are
   New Celtic Monasticism for Everyday People (Mayhew Publishing)
   High Street Monasteries (Mayhew Publishing) and the yearbook *Waymarks for the Journey* (Mayhew Publishing).
His next book will be *Brendan's Return Voyage – a New American Dream: Indigenous, Post-colonial and Celtic theology* (Wipf & Stock)

The Community of Aidan and Hilda UK website is www.aidanandhilda.org